How to Adopt a Child

How to Adopt a Child

Your step-by-step guide to
adoption *and* parenting

Louise Allen

Vermilion
LONDON

1

Vermilion, an imprint of Ebury Publishing,
20 Vauxhall Bridge Road,
London SW1V 2SA

Vermilion is part of the Penguin Random House group of companies
whose addresses can be found at global.penguinrandomhouse.com

Copyright © Louise Allen 2021

Louise Allen has asserted her right to be identified as the author of this
Work in accordance with the Copyright, Designs and Patents Act 1988

First published by Vermilion in 2021

www.penguin.co.uk

A CIP catalogue record for this book is available from the British Library

ISBN 9781785043444

Printed and bound in Great Britain by Clays Ltd, Elcograf S.p.A.

The authorised representative in the EEA is Penguin Random House Ireland,
Morrison Chambers, 32 Nassau Street, Dublin D02 YH68.

Penguin Random House is committed to a sustainable future
for our business, our readers and our planet. This book is made
from Forest Stewardship Council® certified paper.

CONTENTS

Part 4: WHAT COULD POSSIBLY GO WRONG?

INTRODUCTION

This book offers a different approach to giving advice and support to potential adopters. I'm not a social worker, psychologist or adoption worker. I am a surviving adoptee of an adoption breakdown, who has now experienced all aspects of the adoption process from the other side as a long-time foster parent of many children. I have, what is called in the trade, 'lived experience'.

These days I foster children as well as writing books about children in the care system. I am also an exhibiting and teaching artist. I was recently asked by the social worker of one of my foster children if I would think about adoption rather than fostering. Because of that experience I began my formal research, which brought me to write this book to fill the gaps I saw in the information available to those considering or going through the adoption process. I also saw the need for more real detail about how the application process works and how to prepare yourself for your adoption experience.

I have dug into every aspect of adoption that my curious, forensic brain could think of. I have interviewed and spoken with adopters, adoptees, social workers and managers, teachers, doctors, nurses, an accountant, barristers, academics, the police and extended family members around adoptions to bring you my honest, real advice. This book provides a comprehensive account of what you will encounter, which will help guide you as you go through the adoption experience, including the legislation, statutory guidance and standards that govern the social care system around looked-after children.

I didn't write my book to please or seek favour from professionals, and I wanted it to reflect the reality of the system, warts and all. I have written this book for you, the adopters, and for your adopted children so that you will stand every chance of your adoption being a success for you and your child. The adoption process is complex and emotionally fraught, so I aim to empower you with advance knowledge of how the system works, the questions to ask and the information to seek – right from the start. I have heard so many times: 'I wish I had known that at the beginning . . .'

THE FACTS

To give you a sense of the adoption system, consider that there are approximately 100,000 children currently in the care system in the UK, and approximately 5,000 of these children are put up for adoption.

In England, in March 2019, figures showed that around:

- 5 per cent of children in care were aged under a year old, 13 per cent of children in care were aged one to four, 18 per cent of children in care were aged five to nine, 39 per cent of children were aged ten to fifteen and 24 per cent of children in care were aged 16 and over
- There were 21,000 adoptions in 1975 and just 5,797 in 1995
- Roughly half of adoptions are by step-parents

- There are approximately 35,000 children living with foster parents and families, a further estimated 10,000 children are in local authority care
- Roughly half of children adopted come from abusive families
- Those children taken into care from the age of six upwards generally wait an average of five years to find an adoptive family
- Approximately one-third of children entering care live in three or more different homes/placements before settling with a permanent family
- Only 10 per cent of foster applicants become adoptive parents.*

That is sobering reading, isn't it?

These facts show the pressure under which the care system is cracking, and the obstacles and battles ahead of you. My mission is to give you the information you need before you need it – so that you are the strongest applicants and best positioned to ensure a strong match and supportive aftercare for your adoption.

WHAT'S GOING WRONG WITH ADOPTION?

Adoption has always been a political and social hot potato – and much more so in recent years. Stuck in a storm of dramatic financial cuts and with experienced governments and adoption charities happy to put out emotional news in

---

* 'Care – The Facts', Become Charity website, www.becomecharity. org.uk/care-the-facts; 'History of Adoption and Fostering', news.bbc. co.uk/1/hi/uk/256128.stm

the media presented as 'poor little children – give them a loving home and here is a few grand for your effort', the system seems to veer further and further away from the children at its heart. Anyone who has children, and many without, will know that a few thousand pounds is nothing in the realistic scheme of things, especially given that many children looking for a new family have already suffered a lot and will require extra support that someone needs to pay for.

Charities can release emotive news to increase funding and laws can be changed but the benefits do not always reach the adopter and adoptee. Governments, one after another, draw up 'new' resolutions to ongoing issues, none of which openly address core issues. For example, David Cameron's 'Speed Up Adoption' in 2015 led to cutting corners on rigour, asking fewer questions and giving social workers less real autonomy. In late 2019, Gavin Williamson declared a new drive to see the hardest-to-place children matched with adopters – but politicians cannot fully appreciate the inherent difficulties with adopted children who have experienced extensive trauma or abuse and have then lived in multiple foster homes or organisations, moving frequently, each time becoming more traumatised and gaining the label of a 'bad child'.

I looked after a seven-year-old girl who had foetal drug and alcohol damage which was so severe that she ticked every box going – ADHD, global delay and more. She had been moved from foster placement to foster placement. While she was with me I informed the social worker that full-time therapeutic support was needed, to start again and unlearn all current behaviours born out of fear and pain. Instead, I was asked to take 'cute' photographs of her smiling and holding a teddy because they were going to put her on the National Adoption Register. I knew that anyone adopting this child would be in for a difficult time, and with little-to-no support because the legal status of adoption means 'you're on your own'. The few thousand pounds that can follow and be part of the package for an adopted child is meant to last their lifetime. (It is the equivalent of a recent fee I happened to see on the invoice of a therapist charging a local authority (LA) for a few sessions of basic therapy.)

Those who are working in adoption or keeping a close eye on it know that as a sector it is way more complex, and that it requires more than throwing a little money at it here and there. The simple fact that colours the entire adoption experience is that adoption is cheaper for the local authority than fostering and other options, because the cost of raising a child is handed over to the new adoptive parent(s) and legally the LA's responsibility for the child ends (though with some exceptions).

Recently there has been greater recognition of the on-going needs of the child, but this is still a struggle.

When I began fostering there was a fluid working relationship between children's social care, the doctors, the police and schools. Now, the culture of children's social care has changed – new battles rage around bureaucracy and changing government legislations. These days social workers have ridiculous workloads, minute budgets and little autonomy. It seems as if social workers are beginning their training younger and without as much life experience. I see good social workers penalised for spending too much time with children, which is costly. Corners are cut and important work is up for tender.

Funds have evaporated, or in my view the money that comes into children's social care does not always go out in a positive way. I see fees to over-priced agencies or consultants who charge enormous rates for services. The problems are systemic and until we, the taxpayers, demand more information and transparency and until the children are placed at the heart of the process, it will continue to die on its feet.

There will always be a need for children to be adopted unless governments deliver better social policy, and I hope that by reading and absorbing this book you and your new children will benefit from a head start. The greed and corruption in this poorly regulated sector, that the rest of society assumes is lovely and fine, breaks my heart and means that it's a daily fight for children to have a place in society where they can be safe, yet alone thrive.

That is why I write about and campaign on behalf of the children and young people and those who care for them, the adopters and foster carers. I wrote this book to give you and your child the best possible start and support on your travels through the process.

WHAT IS COVERED IN THIS BOOK?

I want to talk about all aspects of the adoption process – before and afterwards in this book. Each adoption is different and each child will have experienced their circumstances differently. There is no one-size-fits-all approach, and nor should there be. It isn't easy placing children into care and it's a myth to think that social workers remove a child from their birth family 'just like that'.

I will explain each stage of adoption and what the reality of raising children from the care system is like. In **Part One: Before You Start the Process**, we're going to look at what you should know before you begin the process, who can apply for adoption and more about what adoption is and the terminology and legalities you will come across. **Part Two: The Adoption Process** takes you through the application stage, step by step, including all the information you will need to provide and when, plus more detail about the matching process and meeting and getting to know your child.

Part Three: Bringing Your Child Home looks at the crucial post-adoption support that is available and how to access and fight for it, and the various relationships you will build with your social worker/s, child's school and other professionals. The arduous application process is over, but this is when other difficulties can set in and being ahead of the game can make this time an entirely different experience if you know what to look out for. Then, in **Part Four: What Could Possibly Go Wrong?**, I want to talk about potential problems with the new relationship and what does and can happen. For many, there will be difficult times and tensions ahead and knowing what to look for and how to handle issues or allegations is fundamental to maintaining and building your relationship with your child. Adoption does not carry a guarantee of success and placement breakdown is a possibility, particularly for an older child who is more likely to have extensive contact with their birth family and have experienced more unstable care prior to joining your family.

You're going to hear lots of terms and many, many acronyms as you take on the world of social care, so I've also provided a list of Adoption Acronyms and Terms at the end of the book for instant support. And I will keep saying this – don't be afraid to ask questions and get clarity when you don't understand something – it won't hold you back to demonstrate your desire to understand exactly what is going on.

There are a number of great charities and support groups that can be invaluable in terms of practical advice and emotional support – plus cold hard cash – to help when needed. I'll include details in the Useful Organisations and Support section at the back of the book, along with other helpful information about where you can find others going through adoption too – from online groups to podcasts and recommended reading. The adoption community is big. Do explore these options and find out what is out there for you.

* * *

There are three phrases that I return to regularly when speaking with those going through or associated with the adoption process:

'Comparison with other families is futile': there is no other scenario that I can think of than parenting where *everyone* seems to have an opinion on how you bring up your child/ren. You have your own unique family unit and you will thrive when you don't compare yourself to others. You have to develop a thick skin and learn to shrug off annoying and unhelpful suggestions from those you love, professionals who have never met your child and complete strangers. My advice is 'go deaf', smile sweetly and – when you are able – scream into a cushion.

'Follow the money': like many public sector services, parts of children's social care have been privatised. It is important that you are aware of this and ask the right questions from the very beginning of the process, because the motivation to help and support you and your child is influenced by the need for these businesses to make a profit.

There are small amounts of funding available to help with your child's emotional needs but local authorities will claim that they have no money due to cutbacks. You need to plan well ahead. Which leads on to:

'Put in your applications for support while life is calm': just as understanding the potentials for financial support and how to work best with the system is crucial, it is also key that, as much as possible, you agree your support at the beginning of the process *before* you take in your child, and then be forceful in ensuring it is put in place. Write all your funding applications with your child's very worst day in mind. Be realistic in terms of your expectations of what could be needed for the obstacles that will arise and challenge language from your LA or agency that may allow them to wriggle out of their responsibility. There will be hoops to jump through and endless forms. The processes can look and feel like they've been designed to make you give up so I want you to be clear from the outset what you are or can be entitled to, and what this means in reality. Knowledge is power.

I do hope that after reading this book you will have fewer surprises on your adoption journey, and that this preserves your time and emotional energy for your child rather than trying to fathom a route through the endless bureaucracy around adoption.

I want everyone reading this book who is thinking about adoption to feel confident, supported and valued, but also to be aware of how the system will work for you and against you. It's really important that adopters understand how the money works or doesn't and what they and their children are entitled to.

I will be thrilled if, after reading my book, potential adopters say, 'We have this, we can do it'.

PART ONE

Before You Start the Process

CHAPTER 1:

What is Adoption?

If you know me and have read any of my other books you will know that I 'say it as it is', especially when it comes to giving vulnerable children the best possible life they need and deserve. Adopters have a lot to do and a magical mystery tour ahead of them but, as I've already said, the adoption process can be emotionally gruelling and the care system is groaning under pressure in terms of budgets, resources and staffing. Sadly, many adopters feel they are abandoned as soon as the ink is dry on the paperwork.

That's why knowledge and awareness are key to a strong and successful adoption. I strongly suggest you start by reading the key legislation around adoption as part of your preparation and learning (more about that later in Chapter 4) and then work your way through this book. This may be the early stages of the process but your child will need support and help, as will you. An overview of the entire process, and the likely issues and obstacles with your particular application, is to your advantage. Many adopters find their involvement with social care and mental health services will stretch beyond the first few months after placement.

ADOPTION HISTORY

Adoption has been around for centuries. From Roman times, it was used as a way of tying important families together or to allow for adoptive sons to manage wealthy estates. Originally it was an informal arrangement between families or within the community, often when children were orphaned or their mothers were unmarried. After the First World War there was a growth in arranged adoptions and only through pressure from adoption societies and charities did the legalisation of adoption come about in the 1920s (as the situation demanded as a result of the numbers of war orphans). Since then, nearly one million children have been adopted.

Young children who came from poverty or were suffering from poor treatment, such as neglect or abuse, would tend to be fostered rather than adopted, and if the children were older they were sent off to work as apprentices or in service. The scope for further neglect and abuse was great.

Once adoptive parents could go to court and secure legal entitlement to keep their child, the state of adoption became more widespread. There were still restrictions around who was able to legally adopt a child – adopters could not be under 25 years old (or less than 21 years older than the child). It was usual for married couples to adopt, though single people were permitted to do so (single men were not allowed to adopt girls except in specific circumstances). At that point, if the adoptive parents died intestate their adopted children had no rights to inherit from their estate – they were not treated as equal to biological children in that respect.

By the mid-1930s, over 4,500 children were being adopted each year – a positive move, but the process was chaotic and potential adopters were rarely interviewed or their homes approved and often references went unchecked. Babies were advertised in the back of newspapers alongside pets and domestic appliances, or were sent overseas without any checks or safeguards. Some 'maternity homes' arranged to have babies adopted for a fee from which the birth mother never benefited. There was corruption and opportunity at every stage.

The process of adoption was shrouded in secrecy, and the arrangement was a closed system which precluded the mother and child from finding each other later in life, leading to distress and many harrowing searches trying to track down lost parents (as shown on TV's *Long Lost Family*). Historically, it was mainly babies who were adopted. They came from unmarried mothers or were orphans. The handover happened and the adopters were not bothered again by the organisation that had arranged the placement. Birth mothers were expected to fully accept the arrangement and the children to feel grateful (if they even knew they had been adopted) and to go through life quietly without questioning it. I believe some of these attitudes still cling to the consciousness of adopters and professionals working in this area today. In our era of social media though, the idea of secrecy is no longer relevant or possible – children can access their birth family with a click of a button.

In the past, adoptive parents were permitted (even encouraged) to rename and redefine their adoptive child's identity and often would go to extreme lengths to convince their community that the baby was biologically theirs. All sorts of shenanigans went on to create layers of lies, secrets and deceit around adoption – it was not spoken about readily, and adopted children were certainly not encouraged to embrace their identity and heritage, but rather be thankful for their 'rescue'. Thankfully those days are over, and I want you to be loud and proud adopters and adoptees.

Since 1975, adopted children have had the same rights as biological children in every family. If an adoptive parent dies without a will, the court will determine each child's share of any estate left by the parent by using the state's probate formula. The court will include adopted children in the calculation and will award the same percentage as biological children. (In 2010, legislation ruled that adopted children might also still have some inheritance rights to the estates of their biological parents.)

Society still has some skewed views about adoption. I feel that adopters are frequently seen as saints or angels, heroic figures who selflessly give up something when, in fact, we gain and there is no heroism involved. That accolade needs to be given to the babies and children who experience loss and trauma and whose lives are recorded on file until they are eighteen.

WHAT IS THE DIFFERENCE BETWEEN ADOPTION AND FOSTERING?

Fostering a child is usually a temporary arrangement (if used as a long-term plan, it is often referred to as 'permanent fostering'). The responsibility for the child in foster care is shared between the foster carers, the local authority and the child's parents. Obviously this doesn't provide the child with the same legal security as adoption, but I've seen situations where it is the right solution for the child.

Adopters can be approved as foster carers while they wait for the legal system to get the necessary paperwork in order for their child to be adopted, especially with babies. It's a reasonably new law that allows the adopters to foster while they wait, so that they can bond with the child as well as creating as little disruption as possible for them.

A long-term foster placement can also be converted into a permanency arrangement. We have done this with one of our foster children. It can only occur if all court proceedings have happened and in the eyes of the court the child is staying in foster care. It also has to be demonstrated that the child and carers are settled and happy. All fostering placements last until the child reaches 18 years. There is then an option called 'staying put' which involves all parties agreeing to the young person staying in the home until the age of 21.

THE CHILDREN

Nearly two-thirds of children in care are aged 10 to 18. The majority live in foster homes, under kinship and special guardianships arrangements (where specific individuals are authorised to care for a child who has been 'taken into care'), in residential homes, 'independent accommodation' (such as hostels, caravan parks, tents, residential schools or family centres offering support to young mothers) and young offenders institutions. (There are also those who fall through the system and who end up living largely unsupported in B&Bs, or worse.)

Only about five per cent of children in care are placed for adoption – about 5,000 each year. Let me explain more. Those children who are selected for adoption are usually under seven years old. They will have been removed from their birth mother/family and it is definite that they will never return home. The courts will have given legal responsibility for the child to the local council (though this is not to be confused with parental responsibility – see below). The council will remain responsible for the child until they are 18 or until an **adoption order** is made, appointing parental responsibility to another (through adoption or special guardianship, for example).

Children 'in care' are subject to a **care order** or an emergency protection order, or are compulsorily accommodated. 'Looked-after' children are those provided with accommodation by a local authority continuously for 24 hours or more – so these include children 'in care' plus children accommodated with the agreement of the parent or guardian. Children placed for adoption are the same children who go into the foster care system, and if an adoption breaks down the child will end up back in the foster care system. There is a preconception that children are somehow divided into appropriate categories but no, they are the same children, it's just the paperwork that's different.

Adoption must be considered as a last resort, and that it can be appropriate only when 'nothing else will do'. To satisfy this criterion, the analysis must show that the needs of the child for permanence and stability within an adoptive family outweigh all of the positive elements identified as being available through ongoing connection with the child's parents or wider family.

Quote from 2013 legal case
(The UKSC in RE B & Re B-S)

You may have started off imagining yourself adopting a healthy little baby, but you will see that shifting your thinking towards an older child from the beginning is likely to increase the chance of you succeeding in a successful 'match' with a child. A shortage of adopters coming forward for years now, partly due to IVF developments and less babies coming into care, has led to difficult-to-place children becoming the norm. Babies who have been relinquished by their mothers are becoming rarer as the rate of teenage pregnancies has fallen, attitudes towards 'young single mums' has changed and babies are more likely to be kept within the family unit. Many who look to adopt initially want to adopt babies or toddlers; if a couple has not been able to have a birth child there is work to be done on their loss and grieving for the child that didn't happen for them before they adopt a child.

The decreasing numbers of babies and toddlers means that older children and sibling groups are more likely to be available. People are less likely to want to adopt older children and teenagers for obvious reasons though – they have been in the system much longer and, while it's hard to hear, they will struggle to settle into an adoption placement easily, especially if they have remained in contact with their birth family. Children's residential homes or foster homes are the most likely options in these situations.

You will also need to think through your idea of what having an adopted child will be like if they still have contact with their birth parent or family. Contact with the birth family is something we discuss throughout the book as there is likely to be contact in most cases, though limited and not sufficient to allow the child to establish or maintain a meaningful relationship.

There are legal protections for adoption parents and it is unlikely that your child/ren's birth parents will be able to undermine your child's placement. Remember that we are all people with our own emotional baggage, dreams and expectations – a regular connection with the child's birth family could be an extremely positive aspect of your relationship with your child/ren so don't think of this as a negative at this stage.

CHAPTER 2:

My Story

My birth mother and father met on the evening of 22 November 1963 outside a TV shop in the square of a small town near Oxford. My mother was on her way home from Girl Guides when she and her friends stopped to join a crowd of people watching the TV footage of the shooting of John F. Kennedy through the window. My father was a taxi driver and married with two children. My mother was 12 years old. He took a shine to my birth mother that night and approached her. She was an only child of elderly, strict parents, and the first generation from a local gypsy community to live in a house; he was a Moroccan Jew. I arrived a few years later. Not many of us get the dream start in life that films and legends portray; I understand I was made on the back seat of the taxi.

My maternal grandparents were not impressed with the pregnancy, though they did know my birth father as he had managed to make himself into a family friend. These days we would call him a 'paedophile' and his behaviour 'grooming'. To this day, when I have tried to talk about my birth father and raised the issue that she was a school child when she met him, a year younger than his youngest child, my mother shrugs her shoulders and says that 'he made me feel special'. She was placed in a mother and baby home in Oxford and I have a photograph of myself as a baby which was taken by the high street photographer next to the home. I am a dark-haired olive-skinned little thing in a white crochet ensemble. I was just about to be thrown to the lions . . .

My birth mother tells of a man from the Children's Department who came to visit her with paperwork. He explained to her that I would be adopted locally in the Oxford area and that she and I would not be allowed to contact each other until I was 18 years old. He told her that I was going to be adopted by a lovely family who had a little boy who couldn't wait to meet me. My new parents were described to my naïve young birth mother as kind, caring and loving.

OPENING MY FILE

After I received my adoption file from Oxford County Council I quickly learned that this was the first set of lies to be told.

I was in my early forties when I received my file. The university where I taught Fashion and Textiles was making a number of us redundant and part of the process was for all staff to be given six free sessions of counselling. I decided to use the time to talk about my own adoption experience. When I got to meet my counsellor, I liked her very much; she was warm and soothing. I remember sitting in her room with my file in front of me. We talked through the reasons why I wanted to read my file with the support of a professional as I did not feel my family would be able to deal with the reality of my past.

Years before I had made the decision not to tell people about my past because I knew that, on the whole, most people I knew would not understand or be able to hear it, or they would perhaps judge me. I had been the subject of gossip and speculation years before when an old boyfriend decided I had been abused as a child because I ended the relationship. I was hopeful that talking through the paperwork would help me understand the chronology of my failed adoption.

It didn't work out as I had expected. Towards the front of the file was a photocopy of a letter and drawing I had made and sent to my birth mother asking her for her help. My life in my adoption placement was very hard, and my older adoptive brother had been removed by the courts for his own safety. The Children's Department chose to leave me there. The letter broke my heart, but not as openly as it saddened my counsellor who sat sobbing as we read through the supporting notes from social workers.

My adoptive mother and father had already been under the spotlight for neglect and abuse of a previously adopted boy, who had been systematically beaten, tortured and starved by my adoptive mother.

Even though the Children's Department was fully aware of the prior abuse they speedily proposed my adoption. A number of social workers and my guardian ad litem (a social worker employed by the Children and Family Court Advisory and Support Service [CAFCASS] to protect and advocate on behalf of the child) objected to the proposed adoption. When I went through my file I was shocked to see so many objections from fellow professionals who described the adoption as 'tricky' and 'dangerous'.

After a year of arguments from within the department, it was decided by the judge that I was to be legally adopted by this couple. In my memoir *Thrown Away Child*, I revealed with much pain the levels of corruption, lies and abuse that became my childhood after the adoption was finally approved.

My brother and I were both subjected to years of abuse and neglect, from being potty trained on a potty filled with bleach to sitting on the kitchen drainer with my feet in the sink while she poured boiling water onto my feet. I still have the scars. I was left up trees, in cupboards, and my adopted brother and I were so hungry we ate potato peelings and grain, the food she kept for the chickens.

My adopted father wasn't a bad man but was weak; she bullied him too. His silence, and the way he turned a blind eye to her behaviour, made him complicit. It also made it difficult for me to trust men again.

I remember clearly the day my adoptive brother was driven away from our home by two social workers when he was nine years old, and how I was not allowed to say good-bye. As I poked my head through the red velvet curtains in the front room I saw his familiar little head in the back of the car moving slowly down the road, and the indicator blinking to go right. My adopted mother pulled me away by the arm, grabbed my chin in her rough hand and said, 'Now my girl, you'd better behave yourself or it'll be you next'.

CONCERNS RAISED

There was no doubt that I was badly let down by the system that was meant to protect me. The papers revealed one lie after another, and showed how the adults, social workers, birth and adopted parents had protected themselves over doing right by me and protecting me from abuse.

Both myself and the counsellor, who could not stop apologising, sat in shock as page after page exposed how our society gave children from challenging starts in life so little. I have always felt that if a child is in or was in care or has been adopted they seem to come with an odour of stigma and shame. So many of us have been treated appallingly by the adults who were meant to keep us safe.

Our treatment did not go unnoticed or unchallenged. In the file were redacted names, addresses and telephone numbers of people who had raised their concerns. After my adopted mother died and I felt that I could revisit some aspects of my childhood, I got in contact with my two cousins who were her nieces. My cousins told me of a friend whose mother and father lived across the road from us and how she made herself ill with worry about us. She had repeatedly reported screams and scared children. She even managed to have my adopted brother round to play with her grandson and while playing in the garden she noticed big bruises and belt marks on his torso so she took photos. In the orchard next door to our house were a number of immigrants living in caravans from Ireland, Czechoslovakia and Poland. I was told that some of them got the bus to the Children's Department to report their concerns about the way we were being treated. No action was taken because they were foreign. There were pages of names, numbers and addresses from concerned neighbours and people in the community, including the headteacher at our primary school who would not back down. That's why my adopted brother was finally removed.

I ran away from my adopted home when I was 15 after being expelled from school and following my adopted parents' last act of violence towards me. I got on a train to Kings Cross. Eventually I came good after many scrapes and falls, fortunately managing to meet some wonderful people who inspired me to not get into trouble with the police or get hooked on drugs or alcohol. Looking back, my behaviour at school, that caused me to be expelled, was a cry for help. It would have been useful if someone had thought then that behaviour is an expression of how we feel, it's communication. We send children on a self-fulfilling prophecy and wonder why.

DOCUMENTARY

Recently I was filmed for a documentary about my life. The producer laid out my file paperwork on my big farmhouse kitchen table for me to be filmed looking through. I had never looked at my file like this before; suddenly as I talked about the paperwork on camera I noticed that all the way through my abuse there was paperwork from the 'Child Protection Officer' who had been repeatedly called out to our house. In his short and concise reports for the file he states 'after another call from [name withheld], I have visited the family and everything looked fine. I have no concerns'. I saw my story and it was even sadder than I had thought.

It was years later after meeting my husband, who had two daughters, and then having my own sons that I ended up fostering children. It was my husband's idea. I resisted for a while. I didn't want to get involved with children's social care but in the end I concluded that I could do it; I know the emotional pain a child with trauma is suffering. I have been fostering short- and long-term foster children for seven years. I never expect to love or be loved by somebody else's child; if it happens it happens because we trust each other and care deeply. I would also rather be in the life of one or two children over a long time and stay in their lives as a friend and support.

CHAPTER 3:

Who Can Adopt?

I feel strongly that the message that adopters can come from all backgrounds can't be shouted about enough – all nationalities, single, married, male, female, homeowner or renting, 'working-class' or 'middle-class', with a range of occupations, straight, lesbian, gay or bisexual. I have met people who have told me that they would love to adopt but feel that they're 'not the type'. The truth is that it really doesn't matter who you are as long as you can be a good parent by giving a child a loving home and being emotionally resilient, flexible and able to manage uncertainty.

Adoption is struggling. The modern children's social care system has taken away such issues as questionable adoptions, but it is far from perfect. I believe that adoption, like so many aspects of raising children, has been over-professionalised – it has been largely seen as an activity for the kind, white, middle classes.

I would love a greater awareness that the adoption process is also open to those who are renting, single or living on disability benefits or with long-term health conditions.

Adoption is also open to you if you are of any sexuality or faith, whether you have natural children already of any age, as long as all parties applying through the process are over 21.

> *I was never interested in interventions so didn't seek IVF or even speak to doctors when we were initially failing to conceive. We chose to go straight to adoption – biology never bothered us.*
>
> Hannah, adoptive mum

TYPES OF ADOPTERS

I have had a lifetime to reflect on my adoption, back when the matching criteria were simply looks and class. It's safe to say that we have moved on since then. All those eligible who enquire about adoption should receive a warm and polite response from the adoption organisation. If that is not your experience then move on to another. Similarly, if at any point during the adoption or beyond you receive negativity because of your sexuality, gender or physicality from professionals or the birth family, you need to inform your organisation or ask for another social worker who should be able to support you. If you feel the attitude is systemic within the organisation I would suggest you try another organisation with more up-to-date thinking.

Today's society is a colourful mix with a variety of family structures, but people still have lots of questions about who can adopt and what might hinder their application. Let's look at some specific cases.

LGBTQI adopters

In December 2002, the law changed which means that whether you are heterosexual, lesbian or gay is not a factor in your right to adopt.

Families For Children

The law changed in December 2002 to recognise the needs and rights of people in the rainbow communities plus the recognition of what these individuals can bring to children. Lesbian and gay adopters are more likely than heterosexual adopters to have come to adoption as their first choice and to feel more equipped to help children with differences.

There is also no evidence to show that children raised by LGBTQI adopters will have a different experience than those adopted by a heterosexual person or couple, or that they may be treated badly or bullied, as society slowly moves away from stigmatising based on sexual preferences and gender identity.

Male adopters

I know male adopters, both single and in same sex marriages, who offer amazing experiences to children and I scratch my head that after all this time why we are not fully utilising this wonderful cohort of people. Men have a huge amount to offer children which is often overlooked because our society is hard-wired to assume that women do the nurturing, and it simply isn't true or necessary. When both my partner (who has his own business) and I were working full-time it was me the school phoned if a child was poorly or something had happened. Men should feel valued and supported for their contribution to a child's life but LAs haven't created a policy and culture that is welcoming and supportive to male adopters. Children's social care can feel like it's stuck in the 1950s, with a focus on women being the primary carers of children. As a woman who has strived for financial and educational independence all my adult life I find this attitude both outdated and disappointing.

Some children needing a safe and loving home may have seen or experienced domestic violence and difficult relationships. They may have a bleak opinion of men that could affect them throughout their lives (I have lived long enough to have seen the cycles of abuse repeated – sometimes it's just easier to resort to what you know). A good male adopter could be the first positive experience for a child who has been abused or neglected. If children do not experience a good male attachment they can grow up with confusion and doubt about half the population. How can this be healthy?

Boys also need to experience acceptance of their 'maleness'. If the day-to-day work of raising adopted children was just left to women, boys would not see themselves in strong male role models. By developing a good attachment to a male adopter, children can explore issues about their birth fathers, their gender identity and know men who understand these needs and serve as excellent models for behaviour and emotional maturity.

> *'Adopted families are the families we are given and need, not necessarily the family we thought we wanted.'*
> Kate, *social worker*

Good adoption organisations will educate, guide and inspire men about how their involvement in a child's life can be hugely fulfilling. Men, you are needed and wanted. If an adoption agency isn't biting your hand off to welcome you with full recognition of what an amazing resource you are to a child/ren, then try another.

I believe it would be helpful if adoption organisations employed more men to deliver the service of social work and independent reviewers, to encourage openness and inclusivity. I have sat in training sessions and observed men remaining quiet as they are very much in the minority. It made me feel sad and ashamed that there's not a suitable environment for men to feel safe about their ideas and feelings. Perhaps adoption organisations could create separate male and female breakout groups during education and training sessions. Why not suggest this to your adoption organisation?

Change needs to happen from the ground up so if you are a potential adopter who happens to be male I salute you and encourage you to be the best father you can be. Children need you.

Transgender adopters

Transgender adopters still face the greatest challenges because local authorities and adoption agencies may have their own prejudices and challenges, connected to the discrimination and oppression that exists in wider society.

The trans adopters and foster carers that I spoke to referred to feeling that they were viewed by the social workers as 'the bottom of the barrel', and that the authorities would refer the most challenging children to them perhaps in the hope that they would 'walk away' or 'mop up' the hardest-to-place children.

I hope this approach is slowly changing. Adoption organisations and their panels need to look at all applicants for adoption as individuals and examine their potential parenting skills. I take the view that the LGWTQI communities have faced some of the greatest challenges in their lives – often from their own families, friends and the community – so they can offer a great sense of humility and understanding of the needs of children who have experienced trauma.

Throughout the various assessment and panel discussion stages, it's important that all parties remember that children are vulnerable to questioning, bullying and teasing for a range of perceived differences – from religion and race to disability and accent. Be prepared to shout out about the offering you bring in terms of understanding the difficult choices and barriers that particularly teenage children face, and how to overcome these and develop a strong sense of identity. Avoiding these issues or hiding them away is not the way for a child to learn to grow and make choices. Adopted young people may become part of the LGBTQI community and organisations should recognise that this is part of their world.

Beware of any focus on this factor in your application that feels overstated or under-supported. The emphasis should be on the potential adopter's ability to support and guide the child through a range of challenges they experience from others, not just homophobic or transphobic bullying.

Finally, your application is confidential and information about you should not be shared without your permission.

Disabled adopters

A health check is part of the adoption assessment process (see Chapter 6), but it is worth noting that physical or mental illnesses do not necessarily preclude a successful adoption application. The emphasis is on the adopter's ability to provide a stable and safe home and upbringing for a child into adulthood, and I urge anyone who has questions to contact their local agencies to discuss this further.

There is also a helpful forum for disabled adopters at Adoption UK (www.adoptionuk.org).

Black and minority ethnic (BAME) adopters/children

There is a disproportionate number of black, Asian and minority ethnic children in the care system, and these children seem to wait longer than white children for a permanent family. There have been attempts from government(s) to eliminate barriers to adoption by removing the legal requirements for organisations to consider 'ethnicity' decisions. I guess the people who proposed this were white, grew up within their birth family, thought this would speed up the process and enable more white families to adopt BAME children.

I am mixed race myself and was adopted by a white working-class family and would argue that recognition of ethnicity is extremely important. Most children who come from the care system with minimal paperwork can spend years of their life trying to negotiate with distant and often uncooperative family members and strangers to learn about and understand their own identity. It isn't fair.

This decision stems from the rigidity of the political correctness around racial and ethnic matching from the 1980s, when it was believed that placing BAME children with families from similar backgrounds was the best way to meet the children's identity needs. The flaw in this thinking was that there were not, and still are not, anywhere near enough BAME families or individuals moving towards adoption, much to do with the ignorance and systemic racism within the culture of adoption organisations.

Mixed background children seem to find adopters faster than Black or Asian children. I guess this is because there are more mixed background couplings than in the past. After discussing this with social workers and adopted parents of BAME children, I feel that today's social workers and adopters are less under the spell and fear of political correctness in pursuing the perfect ethnic match, because with adoption there is no 'perfect match' – with all matches there is an element of the unknown. It's not a perfect world and sometimes the predominately white children's social care system can get stuck on 'perfect world' ideals around sensitive areas such as race and ethnicity when I believe case by case is the best approach, with high-quality support.

I would be sad if potential white adopters held back from adopting BAME children because the adoption organisations had not clarified and promoted their position on diversity. As potential adopters you need to make your own position clear to the adoption organisation and specify that you are interested in a BAME child.

A number of potential adopters revealed to me that they see racism as an overwhelming subject and feared feeling patronised by professionals for not having enough insight into race and ethnicity. I see this as a window of opportunity for adoption organisations to offer education and training in heritage, culture and how to support a positive sense of self for the child/ren to adopters. Also, adoption organisations should be doing more to recruit more diversity in appearance and culture in their staff to encourage more adopters from BAME backgrounds to come forward.

If you are looking to adopt a child from a BAME

background my heart sings. It would be a good idea to look at the demographics in your community to work out where you could seek guidance, support and friendship to support your child's heritage and identity. Request post-adoption lifelong support for your child. Ensure that this is agreed at the start of your journey and that the language used by your adoption organisation does not enable them to wriggle out of their obligation further down the line.

A quality adoption organisation should offer high-quality education and training to overcome concerns in this area. If you are from a BAME background and English is not your first language then ask for an interpreter; a good organisation will be more than willing to comply.

CHAPTER 4:

Adoption Law and Language

When you begin your journey to adopt a child, you will rightly be focused on the immediate needs and requirements of the adoption process and all the anxieties and excitement that will bring. The aim of all your hard work is to bring your child home and begin your lives together, but first understanding the process and the responsibilities of those involved in the process and their relationship with you is hugely helpful.

WORKING WITH AN AGENCY

One of the simplest ways to dive into your research is to find your local authority (LA) adoption team or local adoption agencies online and look for upcoming introductory sessions or talks – most areas tend to hold regular adoption information evenings or meetings for those who are interested. There's nothing better than getting an overview at this stage, including the chance to make contacts and get a sense of local organisations that may be able to advise or help you.

The journey to adoption will likely start either with you approaching your local statutory adoption agency, your LA, who will send you to your area's Regional Adoption Agency (RAA) or you may choose an independent Voluntary Adoption Agency (IAA/VVA). You are going to come up against a huge amount of information (and acronyms) over your journey. (I have a list of Adoption Acronyms and Terms at the back of the book so that you can easily check your understanding.) There are three main routes to adoption:

Local authority (LA)/Regional Adoption Agency (RAA)

Your LA is responsible for looked-after children in your area, including fostering and adoption, and overseeing family-finding and children in care (up to the point where adult social services takes over). The UK is split into regional adoption agencies (RAAs) by area, whereby the LA retains responsibility for cared-for children, and the RAA takes responsibility for family searching and the adoption process and support services across a group of counties/area. Details of all the RAAs in the UK are in the Useful Organisations and Support section at the back of the book.

Independent Adoption Agency (IAA) /Voluntary Adoption Agency (VAA)

These are independent not-for-profit agencies (generally smaller than statutory agencies) that work with RAAs across the country to match looked-after children with those looking to adopt. VAAs can also work with specific circumstances, such as service families or harder-to-place children or sibling groups. I have known a few adopters who have used a VAA because of special features to their adoption, such as a family who used a Catholic VAA or a military family who used a military VAA.

Non-agency adoption

This is the name given to private adoptions where the adopters have not been through an adoption agency, such as a foster carer's adoption of a long-term foster child, or adoption by relatives of the child or step-parents. (Step-parents often go directly through a family solicitor, though they would also be expected to go through the adoption process of scrutiny and references.)

We'll look more fully at how these operate in Part Two and Part Three of the book, but it's helpful to differentiate them at this stage.

TYPES OF ADOPTION

Open and closed adoptions

You'll hear the terms 'open adoption' and 'closed adoption' used often in the early application stages. Quite simply, an **open adoption** is where information about the child's identity and parents is open knowledge, and contact with the birth family on some level is usual. **Closed adoptions** mean that information about a child's birth family and circumstances is confidential and usually unavailable to the adoptee *and* adopter/s. (Closed adoptions can be helpful if the birth mother is at risk of abuse or if it is felt that this is the most healing prospect for all parties to the adoption.)

Most adoptions these days are 'open adoptions' – about 95 per cent – because there are fewer babies being born to young/teenage girls and the children being put up for adoption are usually older. Some children will be adopted by their foster carers, relatives or a step-parent.

Open adoption can be the best option for an older child. Often older children have been in regular contact with their birth family and it may have been decided in court that a continuation of contact will be best. As a foster carer, open adoption can look and feel like a long-term foster placement, yet as a legal adoptive parent you have more input over how and when your child has contact and, if you feel that it isn't working well for your child, you can take the decision back to court.

Mediated/'semi-open' adoption

You will also hear of a **'mediated adoption'**, which is effectively a **'semi-open' adoption**. In this situation, there is communication with the birth family, perhaps cards and letters through a third party such as a lawyer or agency, and/or contact through visits. This communication is always non-identifying, so no details of names or geographically identifying information are available. The contact is 'mediated', hence the name, by the social worker, adoptive parent or official means. This is the most common and preferred form of adoption as it allows the child to develop a healthy relationship with their birth parents, but it requires supportive management to empower the child to understand their early life history and make plans for the future.

Semi-open adoption allows adopted children to have access to their parents later in life, which is beneficial for many reasons. As their birth parents are just a letter or email away, there is the option of the child opening up a relationship with them as they grow older, when they are perhaps more emotionally robust and able to cope with the relationship.

It also allows the birth parents to contact the adoptive family or child later in his or her life if something comes up, like a newly learned medical condition or death in the family. The child will gain the opportunity to know more about their biological family's genetics and history too, filling that void so many adopted children feel in their lives without having full contact, giving satisfaction to the child that they have an identity other than yours. Without semi-open adoption, this contact could be severed and it could be difficult to locate them in the future.

After speaking to a number of adopters whose children have this arrangement, the main advice is to see how it goes. It is called 'mediated', and if your child feels unsettled because of the contact then you can pause or slow it down for a while. Both sides need to understand that the child comes first.

With all adoption types there are pros and cons. Throughout your child's life there will be ups and downs with their birth family, trust me on that one. I have looked after enough children to have witnessed both great love and joy from a child to a birth parent to utter loathing and disdain. Sadly, I have seen too many children hang on to what can seem negative contact and a damaging relationship with a birth parent or family member. Having a birth family anywhere can be like a load of ghosts haunting you, and your child will need to find what works for them.

See how things go, take your time and watch and listen to your child. But before you embark on any contact you will need your child to have settled into your home and your care. This will take as long as it takes, so think carefully about how the idea of contact early on in your new placement will affect your time and experience of attaching to your child.

Fostering to adopt

This involves placing young babies with potential adopters who have also been approved as temporary foster carers while decisions are formally made about the child's future within the family court process.

This is now standard practice with young babies. Babies need consistency and the adopters often benefit from living with the child from a young age. Adopters who are adopting a baby where the outcome decision is as certain as it can be are approved as foster carers to look after the child as parents until the legal decision and paperwork have been concluded. One of the biggest problems in this situation is drift; if cases in court drag on and the child/ren get older and distressed because they either feel that no one wants them or both child and adopters live in uncertainty.

Adopting from foster care

A child can be adopted by their foster carers or by another adoptive family who have come forward via the LA or an adoption agency if the birth parents' rights have been terminated by a court (see Legal Documents and Terminology, see page 43) and the child has been placed in the care of the LA. If you convert from fostering to adoption you need to understand that the LA won't be part of the relationship anymore. The child is totally yours by law.

Overseas adoption

You can also adopt from overseas if the child cannot be cared for in a safe environment in their own country, and there is evidence that moving the child overseas is in its best interest.

Intercountry/international adoption must still go through your local authority or a VAA in the UK to be assessed in this situation. You can't just pop on an aeroplane and walk into an international adoption centre or orphanage without working with your local authority or an adoption agency in your area first (even if you are Madonna or Tom Cruise). They will work in partnership with the overseas adoption agency and prepare your paperwork. The process is similar to adopting a child from home but you may be asked to pay a fee.

LEGAL DOCUMENTS AND TERMINOLOGY

I will preface this by saying that I have no legal training at all – but I have seen the legal process for adoption from all angles. No one can prepare you for the number of processes you will need to go through and the endless forms you will have to fill in during your application and to support your child/ren afterwards. It may seem a test of your commitment and endurance. During your child's life with you, there will also be endless meetings with professionals – from doctors and social workers to members of your child's educational support team and possibly a number of different specialists. Your main role is to know what you should be expecting and asking for, and stand your ground and ensure that your child/ren's needs are genuinely placed at the centre of discussions. (I have taken photos of a child with me and placed the pictures face up on the table to remind everyone why we are there when I want to ensure that the focus remains on the best for the child.)

This book isn't long enough to show you the volume of

information held in documents about the laws around adoption and your and your child's rights. I can't say enough about how important it is to understand the legal framework for adoption in terms of knowing your rights and those of the child in adoption, and being able to quote the law when you need to defend those rights. So many people have said to me; 'If I could start my time again when I was at Stage 1 of the process, I wish I had read all the legal frameworks, guidance and standards for adoption'. You will see and hear 'National Minimum Standards' (NMS) discussed a lot and whatever the issue and concern for your child you can be sure that it fits within an NMS. When you find yourself scratching your head wondering why a decision has been made about your child that you feel is bananas you can check the relevant NMS and work from there to negotiate a better outcome for your child.

So many adopters have said that they wish they had known this information at the beginning, and definitely post-adoption when needing to agree post-adoption support.

I recommend starting with the Children Act 1989 (yes – the legislation is more than overdue for revisiting) plus the 2002 amendments and the Children and Families Act 2014, and then look at the guidance subsequent to that, which fills in much of the detail around the interpretation of the law. It won't be an easy read unless you're used to perusing legalese, and this is another way in which the process disadvantages those who are sidelined by the formalities involved in adoption. I recommend printing out the documents and taking time to read them slowly over a few weeks to digest the information within. Also see Useful Organisations and Support for details of where to find summaries of the legislation, legal guidance and case law around adoption. Note that there are separate legal frameworks for adoptions in Scotland, Wales and Ireland.

I advised one couple going through the adoption process to be fully aware of the laws and NMS. At first, they didn't get around to it, then, because I would not let it go, they read the documents and when they came out of the Adoption Panel after a very positive experience one bashfully said: 'I think we knew more than the panel'. Basically, if you know the law then no one can pull the wool over your eyes!

It's standard practice for savvy adopters or foster carers to have read these documents and to quote them when advocating for their child. Everyone adopting should read these before they begin to talk to the social workers to ensure that they know the boundaries and rights for their children and themselves before and throughout the adoption process. I think having documents like these keeps everyone suitably on their toes in terms of the moral gravity of adopting a child.

We'll cover all of this in Part Two of the book when we talk about the stages of the adoption process in detail. Read on for some of the common terms you will come across and need to understand (remember the list of Adoption Acronyms and Terms at the back of the book too).

Care order

Local authorities have first access to babies and children coming into the system, who will most likely have come via the social services child protection team. A care order transfers legal responsibility to the LA when a child is taken into care under Section 31 of the Children Act 1989. (An interim care order can be made by the courts while a final decision is being made about the future care of the child.)

Adoption placement order

A placement order is a court order authorising the LA to place a child for adoption with any prospective adopter of its choice. Therefore, a placement order follows a care order (or is made if the child has no parents/guardian). Generally parental consent is required, though the courts can proceed without in particular circumstances (i.e. if the child's welfare requires the adoption as section 52 of the Adoption and Children Act 2002), and this can be obtained at the same time as a care order in specific circumstances. Note that birth parents are usually kept informed of their child's circumstances at this stage – they are still the child's parents and retain parental responsibility.

Adoption order

The adoption order is the paperwork at the end of the adoption process that cuts all ties between the birth parent/s and child, so that the adopter become the child's legal parents for life. Parental responsibility formally shifts to the adoptive parents from the birth parents.

Parental responsibility

'Parental responsibility' begins with the names on the child's birth certificate, which could be one or both biological parents. Hence, a biological father does not need to consent to an adoption or care order if his name is not on the birth certificate. In most cases, all those with parental responsibility will be required to consent to an adoption order.

BIRTH FAMILY CONTACT

This is another area with a huge variation of circumstances that we will cover further as we discuss the stages of the adoption process, but I thought a quick overview at this stage would be helpful, as you gain a sense of the many questions you may want to ask at the early stages of the process.

Contact with birth parents (sometimes called 'family time') is determined by social services, courts and foster/adoptive parents. It tends to be either 'direct' (meetings and phone access) or 'indirect' (non-contact such as letters). Contact with the birth family is likely to be limited and not sufficient to allow the child to establish or maintain a meaningful relationship. Again, it is important to understand what adoption will be like if your child has some level of contact with their birth parent or family.

Remember that the barristers and judges will have decided on a plan for the child. Sometimes this can feel deeply frustrating when, as with so many legal decisions about a child, those making their life-changing arrangements have probably never met them. I have felt the sting myself when you are working hard to build a relationship with a child and you're told that the child will have more contact with their birth family.

Unlike with fostering, a child's adoptive parents will have input into how much and when contact will take place. Initially this will have been decided by the courts or with the social worker but, as time goes on, the social worker will step back from this level of involvement as the adoptive parent is the legal parent. If you, the adopter, feel that contact is benefiting your child then you can plan other sessions. It could be an extremely positive aspect of your relationship with your child/ren. Remember also that contact can involve communication with siblings, grandparents or other relations who have a bond with the child. ('Contact' can also be with former foster parents.)

We'll look at this again later.

CHAPTER 5:

Other Questions to Consider

When you begin your adoption journey you will begin to see and feel the difference between people who look after other people's offspring and the old traditional model of family that still clings to the awareness of our society. When I was a child I knew I was adopted, and I noticed my difference. Unlike my experience, which was pretty awful and a good guide as how not to do adoption, I would have loved to have lived with a family who were confident in their own skin and to feel that my adoption was a triumph. It isn't helpful that we are reminded of our differences with the common sayings such as: 'blood is thicker than water' and 'you only have one mother' that we grow up hearing, even from those working in adoption teams. I think these statements reveal just how poorly our society understands the feelings and circumstances of children in the care system and those who look after them.

But I do have some key questions that it might be helpful for you to think about as early in the process as possible – questions that will help you to identify what adopting a child feels and looks like for you, and perhaps your family. What do you think will be easy and what will be difficult? What type of parent do you want to be, and what kind of parenting are you expecting your child to need most? How do you feel about adopting a child with significant emotional or physical disabilities? What do you remember most about your own childhood?

I hope the following pages will help you to develop your thoughts around the matching philosophy that will enable you to see the shift needed by you, your partner and family to understand what adopting a child will mean.

FINANCE AND WORK

On the whole, one parent is expected to be able to take time out of work when a child is placed with you. The time you spend with your new child is essential to your future attachment so you will need to plan carefully and factor this in.

When you are assessed for adoption you may be in full-time employment. If you are a couple you could have two incomes coming into your home, you may even have savings. This is good news but in many cases the children we adopt require extra support, and sometimes one or even two parents can have to give up or reduce work to look after their adopted child. When you adopt you take full financial responsibility for your child and that includes the challenges too.

Think about these possible scenarios before you apply to adopt and assume that the LA will make applying for post-adoption funding as difficult as it can, hoping that many of us will give up and fund our adopted children ourselves. I take the view that if you are entitled to funding then you must apply for it. Working with your school and social worker to manage this part of adopting a child will be key. Make sure you and your family are secure.

As an adopter you gain parental responsibility for the child, and this includes being financially responsible for them so an adopter is entitled to the same benefits as other parents, for example: parental leave, child benefit, tax credits, disability living allowance and carers allowance. There is more about adoption pay and leave in Part Three, where I discuss the financial and legal arrangements when the adoption is confirmed and potential support afterwards.

Your local authority may offer further financial support, if, for example, your adopted child has additional needs, and this should be discussed as part of your child's support package prior to adoption (see Chapters 6 and 9). Everyone around the child needs to be included in contributing to the support package, it will speed things up and broaden the scope. Sharing knowledge, information and costing is crucial for making this work well.

Applying for funding can take months or sometimes longer, so start early. It's all about gathering evidence that demonstrates that your child has extra needs and that you suspect your child will require that additional support.

I have seen well-adjusted adopted children transform into teenagers with colourful and interesting challenges that you were not prepared for. No one knows how any of our children will turn out and we can only do our best, but support down the line should be discussed and secured from the beginning.

PARENTING SKILLS

What is a 'parent' to you? What qualities do you want to embody as a parent? Our childhoods are a big part of who we are now, and who we were as a child is relevant. As is the parenting we received. You may already have a biological child, or this may be your first parenting experience. I think how we were parented seeps into how we parent our own children; my experience certainly serves as a continual reminder as to how not to do it.

Most important is that you feel able to open your heart to your adoptive child for who they are. If you still have difficult feelings around having a biological child, then do seek out support to talk through these feelings before the adoption process begins; you are pushed to address these issues in the assessment stages, especially if you are hoping to adopt a baby.

Think of those close to you whom you want to be part of your child's life – siblings, friends and extended family can all be role models and provide extra support. Ask yourself who was important to you outside your close family when you grew up. You may have been moved by the kindness of a neighbour or friend. Who were your role models? Who inspired you? Those who moved us to action in our own lives and to do good need to be remembered and are key to understanding our own identity, which is constructed from many influences. Understanding how the environment in which we grew up has shaped us is helpful in knowing what will be important to us as a parent.

Boundaries and opinions

I am fluent in dockyard language and enjoy a good blast of rude words. I usually do this alone but occasionally my children have heard me. I have heard them too. If you are a family who refuse to have bad language or blasphemy in your life you need to ask yourself how you will express yourself when you are hurt or angry. Many of the children who come into care will bring with them their own culture, beliefs and colourful language, and this is just one example of when your views of parenting will be challenged by the child you adopt and their upbringing.

When I was younger I was told never to talk about money, religion or politics. I find these subjects deeply important and exciting to talk about and feel disappointed if conversations do not explore these subjects. I grew up unhappily in care and I think when you have experienced adversity you want to understand the world and only through examining these subjects are we helped to do that.

In my role as a teacher I have learned that children and young people who have experienced trauma can engage with big concepts far easier than the minutiae of life such as 'tidying your room'. Religion and faith is another area that brings much interest and challenge. As adults it's up to us to furnish our children with knowledge and awareness. (Note that social workers are not allowed to express their personal, political or religious views.)

I feel we are moving towards a generation of young people who will uphold strong views regarding identity, economy and the environment. Your child may become a vegetarian or vegan and they may join a political group. You will find clashes in your belief systems and that's fine, but it would be sad if that were a reason for an adoption breakdown. As adults we need to teach our children the skills around developing personal beliefs *and* listening to other points of view.

When I walked home from school with then my five-year-old, he reflected on the assembly that had taken place that morning. He looked at me and said, 'Who created God?' Embracing new knowledge and answering questions as best you can make our days more interesting.

Part of adoption is pulling on our current knowledge and experience to prepare for the future. We need to be open-minded and demonstrate that we can positively support our child no matter who they are and what their identity ends up as. These are exciting times for our young people and your prejudices and preconceptions should be explored by the time you get to the matching process.

Are you willing to keep looking, learning, and reflecting? Being curious about your own and your child's behaviour will enable less conflict and better solutions. All behaviour is communication.

CHILDREN OF DIFFERENT AGES

The average age of a child in care is 7.7 years old. Babies are usually adopted quickly, and sometimes with competition. Children seven and over are less appealing to most adopters because originally the adopter's dream was to have a baby or toddler and build their family from there – older children tend to be less appealing, especially teenagers.

However, there are significant advantages to adopting older children or a sibling group. If you adopt an older child the process can feel different because the child will actively take part in the process. They will speak for themselves and have formed views and opinions, and this always excites me. I have known adopters who have been determined to adopt a baby but after seeing a photo of a sibling group, or an older child with disabilities, something switches in their brains. Children and young people, even into their twenties, need a family and a sense of belonging. I struggled with this for years until I had my own family. We all need someone to know us and remember us. Adopting an older child who is already in foster care can also be much quicker than waiting for a baby or toddler, and much of the administration and legal events will have already happened.

Another positive is that most older children in care will have had medical assessments and any medical conditions likely would have revealed themselves and treatment would be in place – though there is the potential clash between hormones, trauma and mental health issues that could need support from you and the support team around them. The same is true for educational development issues.

If after three months you have no referral/potential matching you can decide to go onto a national or regional adoption site and you could find yourself looking at adopting a child from anywhere in the country. Sometimes children have to be placed across the country for safety, or perhaps they have needs that require specialist adopters who are thin on the ground in their area. I know a family composed of two sibling groups plus birth children. One sibling group came from Manchester and the other from North Wales – apparently the accents in the house had gone crazy and were all merging into one! Both placements involved children being removed for safety but the adoptive parents had worked in the police and child protection and could manage the risk. Some adopters may find the risk of troubled birth parents looking for their children too much but others are naturally drawn to these situations. All adopters will be different.

Remember that none of us knows what truly happened to our children, how they really feel and what trauma they may have experienced. We often can't know if a child has experienced particular types of abuse or neglect, or if a specific parenting approach will be most suited to that child's needs. It's also naïve to have conversations around sibling groups where there is a generic assumption that they all experienced the same hardships in the same way.

Each child will have grown up in different environments with different potential for toxic impacts on their development in terms of their individual neurobiology, psychology, attachment and their expectations for the future. As future adopters you need to think beyond the knowledge of your future child's maltreatment and that their 'issues' will automatically lead to negative outcomes for you all.

HOW A NEW ARRIVAL WILL IMPACT ON YOUR OTHER CHILDREN

Families are not as they used to be. They can be an ensemble of adopted, fostered, birth and step-children. I have a blended family and would not change it for the world.

If you are considering a new adoption and have other children in your home, careful planning is needed. Children who have grown up and left the nest also need to be consulted. It's not just you raising this new child, it will be your family, friends and community.

The social workers who are with you through the assessment and matching stages will spend time independently with your other children. They will ask how they feel about a new addition, as well as look to understand the individual child and how the dynamic will work. Some of your children may be step-children, fostered, adopted or be your birth children and I would worry about the impact on the foster child mostly, because it could be a reminder of their feelings of rejection. Reports from schools may help get a sense of what the other children feel about a new addition to the family. This is where LAs and adoption agencies often differ. I have learned that support beyond the new child, is on the whole, much better with agencies.

WHEN DO YOU TELL YOUR CHILDREN?

I believe the most essential part of a successful adoption is that your existing children be part of the matching process. An important consideration is how much to tell the children and when. You know your children and you know what they will hear and how they will hear it. Because the adoption process can have delays and bumps in the road, it would be wise to not inform your other children of the stresses and strains that you are experiencing. Your children will be excited and would benefit from not being involved with adoption bureaucracy. It may be worth delaying deeper conversations about their new sibling until you are closer to the end of the process.

AGE GAPS BETWEEN CHILDREN

Considering the age gap between your children is important. Adopted children will come with emotional baggage, both known and unknown, and every child is different. You know your children and can have some insight into how they will manage sharing you with a new child who may demand a lot of your time.

In their marketing, LAs and agencies may promote good matching and you need to pin them down on this essential. When I began living with other people's offspring there was a rule of a two-year gap between existing children and a new child. I have struggled with this as I learned that children who have experienced abuse, and some who have not, have different emotional ages. I have looked after 14-year-olds who feel happier and connected with my eight-year-old. They enjoyed playing together because my new child hadn't had the experiences of play as my secure birth child took for granted. Also children will attach themselves to other children at different times for various reasons. I take the view when I observe my blended family that they transition through each other, but the connections become stronger as time goes on. They may not get on, just like adults don't always get on, but I don't believe their relationships should be forced. They will find their way and initially you will most likely be the main person in your new child's life.

Research evidence shows that giving each child their own physical space is advisable, and all the children's emotional ages should be factored in. Agencies generally prefer the adopted child to be the youngest in the family, so as children placed for adoption are usually not babies, adoption agencies may prefer your youngest child to be nearer three/four years of age or older before you make an application.

A larger age gap could make it easier for each of the children to feel that their place in the family is secure.

Maybe your existing children will be more mature and better able to support and understand the needs of their new adopted sibling.

You know your children and remember, shortcuts or hasty decisions are likely to come back and bite you. Don't rush the adoption process if you have any concerns.

BEDROOM SPACE

Most good LAs and adoption agencies will only allow an adoption if your new child has their own room – a place of their own. You won't know what's happened to your new child in their past – they may require a particular light on or off or furniture placed in a particular way, to help them feel safe and settled. I have prepared a beautiful room for a child then found they wanted it completely different and were not impressed with my design ideas. They need to feel comfortable and secure in their *own* private space.

When your child is ready, work together to create their room; it's a wonderful way to connect. Your child may not understand your standards or know what a tidy room should look like so be gentle and remember you both need to attach and not fall out over the state of their bedroom. If occasionally turn a blind eye and shift the priority of what's really important, you will feel happier.

I have one child who would prefer to live in squalor, or that's what I thought. I held back, took my time and thought about their past life and wondered if the mess was their safe place. Over time – some years – we have worked together. The room no longer looks like it has been burgled, and more importantly, I have learned not to inflict my views of what a lucky child they are to have a lovely room and my child has stopped freaking out with the stress of it all.

THE WIDER FAMILY

The adoption process largely does not allow for the education of the hearts and minds of grandparents and other relatives and friends who will be a significant part of your adoptive child's life, so this is something that you need to think about early on.

When I told my limited family that I was going to foster and adopt children, the response was disappointing. I remember feeling excited and worthy about the decision to embark on the journey of caring for children who have experienced trauma but I realised quite quickly that if you decide to adopt or foster you can rapidly exist in a strange and weird place. You become one of those people that other people think are mad. Women holding their own children looked at me saying 'I could never do it'. Once you are sure in your own mind and have gone through the various stages of your own acceptance with your decision then stick to it like glue.

I recommend that you include supportive family and friends as much as you can and deal with any pushback maturely and calmly. Most adopters I spoke with reported that their friends and family warmed to the idea and some were blown away with the new commitment and understanding forming around them, but it can take time. Talk to your LA or adoption agency about opportunities for the extended family and family friends to attend information evenings and point them towards books and online research so that they can discover more about what you are going through in their own way.

Your mission as adopters is to educate them into understanding that they will need to throw the rule book out and write a new one. Your friends and family will self-reference – they will compare your child with their own experiences unless you are one of those amazing families that I have met where at least half of the family have adopted or fostered children (usually because they grew up with it and understand it). I beg you and them never to compare your child with another; your child is unique and is joining your family for life. Help build a strong foundation for those extended relationships – you will need that support and your adoptive child will benefit from differing generations and personalities around them.

> *Our adoptive parents wouldn't let us be friends with other children who had been adopted or fostered. They were worried that we would all traumatise each other. My husband grew up in care and we totally get each other. I wish I had known more children like me when I was young – I wouldn't have felt so alone and different.*
>
> *Lottie, Adoptee*

This will be a lot to take in, and I am not going to pretend that bringing up children from care is easy – it's challenging. But parenting is never straightforward and I think there is more scope as an adoptive parent to be an amazing parent. Your child, whoever they are, will be amazing and will give you adventures you never expected.

PART TWO

The Adoption Process

CHAPTER 6:

The Five Stages of Adoption

I'm so excited for you choosing to start your adoption journey – these children need you.

As you begin the formal process, you will have done your research and should feel ready to be examined, tested and supported by your adoption team. There will be ups and downs in the process, and you will learn more about yourself, your strengths and weaknesses over the coming weeks and months. But remember that your adoption team is behind you and the process is about matching you with the most suitable child and preparing you to become the best parents possible.

In this section of the book, I will take you through the five stages of the process (pre-stage plus stages 1 through 4), then will look in greater depth at your relationship with your social worker and adoption 'team', matching, meeting your adoptee and that child moving in with you.

The following steps form the process:

> **Pre-stage:** Reading this book and research around adoption
>
> **Step 1 (usually two months):** Submit Registration of Interest form with one chosen agency and go through initial checks (references and medical and police checks)
>
> **Step 2 (usually four to six months):** Preparation/Training and Assessment and Adoption Panel
>
> **Step 3 (time variable):** Matching for you and the child
>
> **Step 4 (time variable):** Approval/Moving in

PRE-STAGE

I recommend you start by gathering information and researching the options in your local area. It's a good idea to speak to anyone you know who's been through the process already about how they proceeded. If you don't already have an organisation in mind then contact your local authority and nearest adoption agencies to see what they offer and to make first contact. Local authorities and agencies will vary in the way they carry out the process and have strengths and weaknesses, but I would suggest you select an organisation that is no more than an hour's drive from your home.

Note that babies and young children will have been taken into care through the child protection team and so will likely be in the care of the LA/RAA primarily. The LAs are keen to recruit adopters and tend to have a good pre-adoption support but adopters have mentioned that some LAs do not have such a strong reputation for robust post-adoption support as other agencies.

Definitely talk to several to see how they make you feel. Start by requesting their information packs and at this stage you can attend adoption information evenings for all options and organisations, prior to deciding which organisation to proceed with. You can only formally apply to adopt with one organisation or agency.

Most of these information events will be similar, and those speaking will likely be giving a very positive view of adoption, so attend a few events to get a variety of stories, and ask if you can meet other adopters in your area or attend any informal groups for adopters so that you have the opportunity to ask more questions of adopters who have been through the system. There may also be online groups that you can attend, too.

Also, ask about the general eligibility criteria with each option to ensure that you meet all their specific requirements. Generally, these will be that you are over 21 and have lived in the UK for a specified amount of time or be a British citizen. Most will insist that you have a spare room for an adoptive child, and some may require you to live within a certain distance of their offices. Having other children will not affect your eligibility, but if you are going through or have gone through fertility treatment, agencies may stipulate that you have ceased these for a period of time before making an application. These are part of the adoption framework, the regulations around adoptions, so there shouldn't be any difference in eligibility between different agencies but, as I discussed earlier, you may feel more comfortable and welcome with certain agencies than others. Each authority and agency will have to work from the framework, however 'interpretations' of support can vary depending on budgets and inclinations/culture of that particular organisation.

You should expect to experience a response to your initial enquiry which is prompt, polite and welcoming. What you want to do here is BIG. If, when you call, they take ages to answer the phone or you are transferred or they are not polite or helpful, then don't be afraid to end the call and move on to another option. Don't be put off if your first enquiries are not as positive as you hoped. Try elsewhere, or drill down into why you are not getting a more favourable response. Your adoption application can only proceed with one agency which is why you need to feel that you're working with the right team.

Look at what the different organisations offer – it's never too early to ask detailed questions, especially when it comes to post-adoption support. Pre-adoption support and funding will generally be in place for children by the time they enter the matching process, so you should be asking about post-adoption support as a distinguishing factor.

Most will usually suggest a visit or a pre-planned phone call with potential adopters (agencies tend to do visits more than LAs, which will likely only visit as part of Stage 1). You may also be offered an invitation to an extra information session where you could meet current experienced adopters. I urge you to accept all opportunities like this.

A visit from the agency can be very helpful in terms of you having the opportunity to discuss your specific circumstances at this early stage and to ask lots of questions.

Remember that adoption is about living with a real family, not a family from a magazine – so a visit to your house can show your half-decorated spare room and your washing hanging on the radiators. This entire journey is about emotions and relationships, not the size of your garden or your proximity to the main road.

You will likely work with several social workers through the adoption process, but my recommendation is to look for a social worker who will help galvanise the trust that is needed between you and the agency or authority.

At this stage, there is no commitment from you – you are exploring the process and options and gaining information without pressure to go further until you have decided that adoption is the right thing for you at this time, and have found the team that you want to work with.

STAGE 1: FORMAL APPLICATION
(TYPICALLY TWO MONTHS)

Once you've decided which route is right for you, the process formally begins with you submitting a Registration of Interest form to your preferred agency.

Registration of Interest (ROI) form

This form is generated by the adoption agency or RAA or VAA, so there is no standard form. It usually requires basic identification information for all members of the household, plus it can require details of earnings. Along with the form, you will usually be asked to provide three referees. You will likely be asked to give details of the type of child you are interested in adopting. The form mainly covers formalities, and any issues would likely have been uncovered during your initial conversation with the agency, so don't worry when filling this in (you will have to get used to filling in a lot of forms over the coming months and years). Once you have submitted your Registration of Interest form, you should receive a formal acknowledgement and response from the agency within five working days.

Preparation to Adopt course

Next, you will probably be invited to a Preparation to Adopt course (or it will be called something similar) which aims to give you a greater understanding of what adoption looks like, and helps you think about how you will be as an adoptive parent and who are the children waiting to be adopted. If you haven't already, this is when you are likely to meet adoptive parents who can talk informally about their experiences and add more depth to your knowledge of what is ahead.

The course is usually a three-day exercise, run by social workers and held over weekdays and weekends. During this time you'll be encouraged to speak up about your own feelings and fears around the adoption process, and also to engage in role play exercises and hear from other professionals around the adoptive system, such as an education or occupational psychologist or senior social worker, as well as other adoptive parents with differing experiences speaking about the reality of the process.

This is also a fantastic opportunity to meet others going through the process and to share your experience. Most people will have the same questions and concerns as you, so this will help you to feel more at ease with the steps ahead and raise the questions you have about the assessment process, the Adoption Panel and matching. You'll get to see the different sides of the adoption process, plus you'll find supportive others and begin your first friendships with potential adopters in the same situation as you.

This course is normally part of the Stage 1 process, though some agencies will do this in Stage 2. Don't be afraid to ask at the beginning for a complete breakdown of what the agency expects to happen and when – there will be differences in how different organisations organise their process.

Police checks

The agency will also carry out checks to ensure there are no concerns about you caring for a child/ren. They will need to do a standard police check – a DBS (Disclosure and Barring Service) – a criminal record check to ensure you are safe to be with children. This is a standard process, which anyone working with children or volunteering with children's groups or in schools will have also been through, so you may already have a valid DBS clearance.

If you have any concerns about what a police check may show, then I recommend starting a conversation about this early in the process – your relationship with the agency and your social worker/s is about trust and working together so it's helpful to be open about information that will be revealed during the process. It is not impossible to adopt a child if you have a criminal record, but it can make the process more difficult depending on the circumstances around the offence.

Medical check

You will also have to get a medical check as the agency wants to be sure that you are sufficiently well, both mentally and physically, to provide a stable and safe home for a child until they reach the age of 18, and hopefully afterwards. Your medical report will be prepared by your GP, and there will usually be a fee charged for the service.

The appointment will include basic health checks such as measurement of height, weight and blood pressure, plus discussions around your general health and medical history. You'll also be asked questions about your lifestyle, including smoking, drinking, diet and exercise, plus any family medical history concerns.

I should note that if you are a smoking household, this may place restrictions on the child you are able to adopt. For example, no child under five with a respiratory condition will be placed with a smoking adopter. General physical or mental disabilities don't necessarily preclude you from being considered for adoption and it is helpful to work with the agency to demonstrate how any vulnerabilities offer crucial strengths to your ability to parent and raise a child rather than cause issues. This report will be sent to the agency's medical adviser, who will review it and may contact other medical professionals if they require further information or clarification about anything in the report.

Again, if you have a health issue, this does not mean you will be overlooked but it may require a little more thought and time. Mental health issues are given careful consideration and, like physical health issues, don't necessarily make someone unsuitable to adopt. Issues are best discussed early on so that all parties are aware of the situation and you can talk through your concerns.

Finally, I would stress that if the health check showed any problems or if you are in less than good health, then please start getting fit at this stage. I can't stress enough how much energy you will need for adopting a child and the stressful times that will happen to all new adoptive families in the first months.

References

You will also be asked for references to help assess your appropriateness to adopt. Again, the requirements here may vary from agency to agency (and possibly come at different stages of the process), but you will generally need to supply:

- A work reference from your current employer (plus previous employer if you have recently taken on a new job or if you work with children/vulnerable adults). Be aware of this if your employer doesn't yet know that you are applying to adopt.
- Three nominated personal referees, who will then be contacted by the adoption team for a telephone interview. (See below.)
- Details of your finances (see below).
- A written reference from your child's school or health visitor, if you have other children.
- A report from your vet about any dogs or potentially dangerous animals in the household (I advise that you do this before you are asked to do so).

Personal references

Your personal references can be anyone who can vouch that they know you well. It may be stipulated that at least one should be a relative and that at least one referee should have known you for at least five years.

Once you have provided your referee details, the social

worker will contact them by phone to discuss you and your application. Always alert your referee first to expect this and have an honest and frank discussion about how and why you are applying to adopt. I also advise you to ask the referees to supply a written reference that is also copied to you – to confirm the content of their conversation and to keep you as part of this process.

I am often asked about who else social workers may wish to contact. If you have any children from a previous relationship, ex-partners must be contacted for a brief interview and a request for their thoughts on this application. If you have concerns about this, talk to your assessing social worker early in the process. If you're concerned about your safety (or your child from that relationship), that will be taken into account. The assessors are, of course, aware that previous relationships may have broken down badly and will balance any information provided by your ex-partner with the other information they have received. Similarly, if you have been in a relationship of over 12 months or a co-habiting arrangement, the social worker may ask to contact these people. In the next chapter, I discuss working with your team and your right to privacy, so discuss any concerns with your social worker as all references will be sought in discussion with you.

Financial information

The other major area of exploration is your financial records. You will be striving to show that you are financially secure and responsible with money in order to care for a child until the age of at least 18, so this could be achieved by showing savings, mortgage/rental payments and earnings. Some agencies will ask for records for the previous ten years.

Discuss these requirements with your social worker as

everyone's situation will be different, especially over the past decade. You could consider asking an accountant to prepare this information for you. I also recommend that you adhere to the minimum requested. The agency do not have the right to access all of your financial records so choose what you show them.

As part of this stage, if you haven't already, you should receive a home visit (sometimes called a Health and Safety visit). Again, this isn't to present an immaculate home. You will likely need to demonstrate a safe home environment for a child plus show the bedroom that would be available.

At the end of this stage, once all of your paperwork and references have been submitted to the agency, your application will be progressed onto Stage 2 if you are accepted by the agency to proceed.

STAGE 2: PREPARATION/TRAINING AND ASSESSMENT (TYPICALLY FOUR TO SIX MONTHS)

If you still want to continue, and I hope you do, you will now enter into 'the work' that is known as the assessment or home study/training phase. This will be all about you and your family.

Once you have been 'accepted' onto the Assessment Stage of the process, your adoption team will support you through the assessment process (see the next chapter for more information about the likely members of your adoption team). You will be appointed your own social worker at this time, if you don't already have a specified social worker for this stage of the process. They will lead the adoption team and be your key contact from now on. We'll talk further about your relationships with your social worker/s in the next chapter, as this is a relationship into which it is worth investing time and energy.

Assessment/Home study

Assessment builds on the process so far and is a two-way dialogue about you and your ability to look after and love a child/ren who has had a tough time. The social workers need to feel that you can offer a potentially challenging child a safe and loving home, and be flexible and creative in your understanding of their changing needs. Remember that this child/ren will already have had to say 'goodbye' to their birth family and probably foster carers too.

You'll be asked to explore how your cultural, traditional and historical beliefs impact on your understanding about parenting a child in their early years, and as they grow older and then move through their teens. Do you feel experienced and informed to predict your child's future developmental needs and outcomes? Are you flexible and agile enough to manage and support your child's changing needs for routine and predictability as new challenges and information come to light? Have you examined the similarities and differences between raising birth children and children through adoption?

These questions and others will be put to you by a good social worker who will want to feel that you are prepared to parent an adopted child. For a good match you need to be genuinely confident about what parenting is and how you think you will do it. I would strongly suggest that you factor into your thinking a lot of flexibility based on structure and boundaries. Remember none of us really knew how to parent until we had a child. But everyone will have an opinion on how you do it; family, friends, strangers and the professionals you meet on the way. You need to be strong and accept that no matter how well prepared you are, there is always the unknown!

This is the stage that some find most intrusive, but by the time you get to this stage I hope you will understand why it's so important, for you and your new child/ren. You will be invited to group sessions to meet other potential adopters, which is a great opportunity to make new friends. You will hear from experienced adopters, foster carers, adopted adults and maybe from a birth parent. In a safe and confidential space you will be able to ask questions and share fears and excitement.

According to guidance, the assessment process should take no longer than around six months. There is no charge for being assessed by a UK adoption agency, unless you are being assessed to adopt from abroad.

CoramBAAF

You will be given homework tasks to help the organisation get to know you and your family, and to ensure that you get to know yourself more clearly. This will be the initial work around matching as you also agree with your social worker your expectations about the number of children you hope to adopt, and their likely age, gender and circumstances.

By the end of this assessment process, your social worker and the agency will have prepared a report known as a Prospective Adopter Report (PAR) on your circumstances and what they consider your strengths and weaknesses as a potential adopter to go forwards to an Adoption Panel for consideration. You will have the opportunity to review the report and hopefully you will feel positive about your prospects after working with the agency to support a strong assessment.

Going to panel

Each agency has its own adoption panels made up of a wide mix of people – from adoptive parents to adults who themselves have been adopted, or perhaps professionals from children's services, health and legal teams as well as members of the local public who are not involved in the adoption process. The panel is supposed to be representative of the process, but also not too formal.

Your social worker will present your assessment report – your PAR – to the panel. Again, there is no specific format that this takes but it will include information about your suitability for adoption plus the type of child/ren you are looking to adopt. You will be invited into the panel meeting. I have been to a few of these and it can be nerve-wracking but it should also feel joyful as you are all working towards finding another child/ren a home.

The panel will ask you questions about your life and how you would potentially deal with challenges in the future.

They will decide whether you should be approved as an adoptive parent or not, but they may also make recommendations about the number of children and their ages based on what they have heard. (This will not fix the final decision – there will be flexibility as no one knows what or how many children will be available once you have been approved). The senior officer (the agency decision-maker) within the adoption organisation, usually called the Independent Reviewing Officer (IRO), will ultimately make the decision as part of the matching process.

If you are not approved by the panel, you can appeal and

take advice on what work you would need to do to try again. Usually the agency social worker and the team in the background would have worked hard to get you to the panel to be approved, and you will have had lots of conversations around what you can do to improve your application for another time.

STAGE 3: MATCHING

Once you are approved by the Adoption Panel, Stage 3 of the process gets exciting and incredible. You are going to be the parent(s) of a child/ren who deserves your love and kindness – my heart is racing just thinking about it.

Your social worker will know the children who are available for adoption, so they may already have a child in mind. Sometimes the 'link' – where a possible match is being considered – has already been made before you were approved at panel ('link workers' can be part of this process). In that case, the child/ren's social worker will be contacted to get their child's profile/details to you swiftly. Everyone should be working together to get things moving – delays can be detrimental to a child who has been waiting for permanence and has been dreaming of a family.

For us matching was an easy process, the social workers did it all. We had of course filled in forms with our preferences to guide them. As we were looking for an early permanence placement we didn't do any of the traditional searching process. We were told of a girl who was looking to relinquish her unborn child a month or so after we finished our training and they thought it may suit our circumstances.

Adoptive mum

There is not a constant supply of children or adopters, so sometimes there may be a wait. If there isn't a child/ren available immediately that fits your preferred/recommended adoption, you and your social worker will begin a search together. As one adopter told me: 'We waited for months, nothing! Then, like buses, our social worker was phoning up saying they were inundated with children coming up for adoption!'. There is no rhyme or reason but sooner or later you will get a link, then hopefully a match.

Matching is absolutely crucial to the success of an adoption, so don't rush or feel pressured at this stage if something doesn't feel right to you. I talk more about matching, background reports and how it works in Chapter 8.

STAGE 4: APPROVAL/MOVING IN

When you do 'find' your child/ren, and everyone is in agreement, the proposal will go back to the Matching Panel (usually consisting of the same people as those who previously approved you on your Adoption Panel so they are fully aware of your circumstances). The panel will study the Adoption Placement Report (prepared by the prospective adopter's agency) in order to consider the match. It's vital to note that this report includes the 'agreement of terms' or Adoption Support Plan (see below).

Once approval is given from the panel, the decision goes to the agency decision-maker who has up to eight working days following the panel to authorise the adoption placement order. Immediately after the decision, a 'placement planning meeting' is arranged to be held as soon as possible. (A date for this meeting may be set in advance of the Matching Panel, but it should take into account the potential eight-day delay.)

The placement planning meeting should not be held until any birth parent consent issues have been resolved.

Before you get to meet your new child/ren, first talk to the people who have been most closely connected to them in their life so far – the foster carers, teachers, the child's doctor and paediatrician, social workers and anyone else who will help you get to know and understand them. Sometimes an agency will arrange a Child Appreciation Day where you can all meet in one go, which is a great event.

Ask lots of questions (make notes beforehand so that you don't forget anything) and feel free to express any concerns you have about the adoption. This is a big decision and it is still not too late to withdraw if you think this match is not right for you and your family.

'Agreement of terms'/Adoption Support Plan

This is the vital window of opportunity in which to tie down the future support you require – financial and otherwise – with the help of your social worker, the child/ren's social worker, your adoption support team and the IRO. Every adopter I have spoken to talks about how important it is to ensure that this part is not skipped over in your excitement to move forwards with the adoption. When you work with your social worker to create the support package, remember to include your school and SENCo (Special Educational Needs Coordinator).

At this stage you will agree what is called your child's Education, Health and Care Plan (annoyingly some authorities call it a EHCP and others an HCP). This specifies any special educational needs of your child, and the provisions that the local authority must put in place with regards to their extra needs.

By this stage, if you haven't already, ensure that you read Part Three of the book so that you understand the support you could and should request to be put in place before the adoption goes forward. Your EHCP/HCP is the start of your journey to stand up for the rights and needs of your new child. I cannot stress enough that this is the time to be realistic about the challenges that will lie ahead in even the most straightforward adoption. Ensuring that the EHCP/HCP represents the full scope of the child's likely future issues is the one thing you can do to protect your new family against the inevitable bumps ahead. This could be the first of many battles with the authorities to get the support you need, so be strong and clear and informed.

> *We were given so much opportunity to ask questions, and with the birth mother too, so I don't feel there was anything we couldn't ask or didn't get an opportunity to ask.*
>
> *Adoptive parent*

Introductions

At last, the time has come for you to meet your child/ren. There will be a planned period of introductions which can last from a few weeks to several months depending on your future child's age and needs. This will include visits to the child at their foster carer's home, and one or more visits to you, likely including overnight or weekend stays.

Though exciting, introductions can be stressful for all involved. That's why careful planning and good communication are important. You should have already met your child's foster carers and they may be feeling as anxious and nervous as you. Remember that this is about the child first – their needs, feelings and emotions. If you and the team around the child rush, impose or fail to read the child then the introduction period may not be as joyful as you all hope.

Your child does not need any surprises so be aware that they, hopefully with this transfer, will see the end of what may have been numerous distressing 'moves' in their life, but they will also be saying farewell to places and people who have been extremely important in their life. The why, what and when need to be clearly understood. Be mindful that 'everyone' will probably have a view about what's best for your child, and emotions can run high.

Early meetings will follow national guidelines but with good relationships there is scope to negotiate and tailor the introductions to meet your child's and your best interests. My advice is to try to roll with it. Everyone wants this to work well and, as with every event where there is a sense of 'committee' organisation, lots of deep breaths may be the best way forwards.

The introductions usually start with a short meeting in the child's foster home, often just an hour (your social worker and/or the child's may be there also, depending on diaries). Over the following days, the time that new parents spend with the child will build up to full days. Initially the foster carers will be very involved, sharing details of the child's routines, needs, behaviour, likes and dislikes, but gradually the child's care will move across to the adoptive parents. A lot of the detail can be chatted through on the phone or shared in an email also. This is sometimes difficult as it can feel very artificial to carry out care tasks in the home of someone who you hardly know but this is crucial for a smooth transfer.

Both you and the foster carers should be mindful that this is a highly emotional time and consideration must be given by both parties. Sometimes foster carers can feel swept aside and their own feelings about the impending adoption ignored. They are important – they may have a wonderful attachment with the child and with patience and wisdom you can learn a lot from observing their relationship with the child. Time spent with your child watching you have a good relationship with their foster carers is hugely beneficial.

When your new child sees that the foster carer has confidence in handing over the intimate and important work such as bathing, dressing and so on to you, that sends a strong message. You will be expected to show that you can deliver on these tasks. It's about trust and your child feeling safe and I cannot stress enough that children, especially children from trauma, do not miss a thing. They will likely be adept at watching the adults around them and looking for signals as to intentions and emotions.

Mid-way meeting

Your social worker will be in touch regularly to check in with you and offer advice and support during the introductory period. There is always a 'mid-way meeting' where everyone gets together to review how things are going and to air any worries or concerns. This is also an opportunity to review accelerating or extending the introductions.

Be aware that all LAs and agencies have a slightly different approach when it comes to the length and format of introductions, which will also vary according to the age and situation of the child/ren you are adopting. To give you a sense of timing, introductions for younger children tend to last around one week.

Do not underestimate how physically and emotionally draining the introductions will be. You will be exhausted – that is normal! Remember to make sure you take some time out in the evenings whenever possible to have some space to yourself and to be able to reflect and recharge before you bring your child/ren home for good at the end of introductions.

Remember this can feel scary at times. I like to compare it to when one of my elder step-children and her partner wanted their parents to meet before the wedding. It is in everyone's best interest to make the introductions as lovely as possible, but also keep a sense of reality. You are aiming to glean as much information as you can about routines, values, rules, roles and expectations, as well as how your child expresses their different feelings, and how they show affection and disapproval. None of this needs to feel like a surprise when your child moves in to live with you if you have taken the time necessary at the introductions stage.

You need to read your child's Permanency Report – the document presented to the court in order to secure an adoption placement order. It's worth remembering that the child's Permanency Report was written by a social worker who had to prepare evidence and information for court. It may not have all the information you need.

Remember that many foster carers are adopters too, and we can be a fantastic source of support and can help your child, no matter how young, develop the sense that permission has been granted for your child to love you guilt-free. Most social workers will encourage you to develop a good relationship with the foster carers moving forward and continue it after the adoption.

Helpful tips for a smooth introduction process

- Food is a good way of breaking the ice and frankly being liked (check for allergies first)! I'm not a natural baker but I try to make or take cakes or biscuits to meetings. The children love it.
- Make sure you have the foster carer's contact details. It may be worth setting up a WhatsApp group so that they can send over images and films.
- Be like a detective and write down everything the foster carer and the child's social worker tell you about your child. Ask them to think of helpful details about the child. It might be a small thing, but I learned through a second or third chat about a child that she liked her forehead tickled in the morning when she is woken up. It makes her giggle and has been a fantastic way to start the day.
- Never be afraid to ask questions. This is your child we're talking about. You will need and want to know everything.
- Include your family in conversations with your child, once it feels appropriate. Answer any and all questions that they have – encourage their curiosity about you and their new home and family.
- Don't exclude pets from the introductions, if you have any. They can be very important for the child and if you have pets, and I hope you do, they can be excellent photographs to leave with your child to feel excited about. I have a few cats and once got a kitten for a new child. I have seen and heard of wonderful relationships developing with pets that I could never have achieved myself.

- If you feel that the relationship is going well, you could ask the foster carer to display your photos in the child's bedroom. Maybe buy the child a new soft toy. You can't buy emotions, but you can plant seeds.

- Remember that the foster carer will have done a lot of work to help your child get to where they are. They will probably have bonded and attached (aka love) your child. Sometimes social workers can be a little brutal with foster carers' feelings, but you don't have to be. They are not competition and at this stage they know your child better than you. If they have other children in the placement include them in all your hellos and good-byes. Make them feel respected and remembered.

- Remember to take photos and gather some mementos ready for later. It's okay to put a picture of your child's foster family in their room and it could help with the transfer. After a while your child may not look at it so much or, as happened with a child I looked after, he put the photos away when he was ready. I put them in his memory box.

- Remember the power of scent, especially with young children. I recommend asking foster carers what washing detergents and conditioners they use and changing to that so that you smell more familiar to the child. Also, think about sleeping with a new teddy for a few days before giving it to the child to keep in their cot or bedroom to help the bond.

- There will be ongoing meetings and phone calls with your social worker about how this is going, and whether you and the child/ren need further support. Part of these conversations are discussions about arrangements for contact with their birth family, if that is important to the child.

- Some agencies hold 'family and friends training' to help those close to you learn about the process and what they can expect and how they can support you and the new arrival in the family. Do take up this offer if possible – the stronger and better informed your support network, the easier it will make the road ahead.
- Finally, never underestimate how saying more goodbyes must feel for your child.

We included family and close friends all the way through the process and had people attend the friends and family training, so they were prepared for what was to come, although no one was actually able to keep their distance and loved her the second she was with us. No amount of training or prep stops this – it was impossible for anyone not to immediately feel she was ours and staying, so thank goodness ours was a happy story.

Adoptive mum

Moving in

Before your child comes to live with you, you will need to register them at your doctors' surgery. Set up an appointment for about two weeks after they come to live with you just to have your child introduced to your GP and a little health check.

Make sure your house is safe before they arrive, especially if you have a crawling baby; they are literally into everything and you may need eyes in the back of your head.

I also recommend your fridge and freezer is full to the brim and extra supplies are distributed throughout your home – for a few days expect it to feel like Christmas afternoon. Discourage your friends and family from visiting for a short while. This is going to be hard for your child who will have said goodbye to people and places a few times already and meeting too many people in one go may unsettle them.

At last the day of your child or children moving in will arrive. Think about how you want this to be, and remember all of your training and conversations and how emotional this may be for your child. A small celebration could be wiser than a party where your child/ren may feel overwhelmed.

Every adopter I spoke to about this day told me that they had not expected to feel so tired. You have been on such a long journey, and have likely travelled through every emotion possible, so don't be surprised if you feel a bit out of sorts and if the day is not the happiest day you expected. The good news is that it's going to be more tiring now you are a parent! (That's why I mentioned getting fit and healthy before you start the assessment/home study stage earlier.) Enjoy some snuggles with your 'new' child – the next stage of your adventure is about to begin.

How is the adoption made legal?

There are certain minimum periods for which the child must live with their adopter/s before an Adoption Order can be made, or, in England and Wales, before an application can be made to the court for one. The precise details vary slightly depending on the country concerned and the circumstances in which the child came to live with the adopters, so research this for your own situation and discuss with your adoption team to be clear of the process. In England and Wales, it is at least 10 weeks, and in Scotland and Northern Ireland at least 13 weeks.

For many families it may take longer and there could be issues of parental consent from the birth parents to be resolved by the court. Once the Adoption Order is granted at an Adoption Hearing, the adoption is permanent and all parental responsibilities for the child transfer to the adoptive family. Now there are no means for any members of the birth family to contest the adoption of the child.

You will be given an adoption certificate which includes the child's new surname and the opportunity to attend a Celebration Day where adoptive families and children meet the judge or magistrate who presided over the court hearing to celebrate the adoption order and have photos taken. The formalities are over, and you are officially a family. Congratulations!

CHAPTER 7:

You and Your Adoption Team

I want to talk a little about those who will support you throughout the adoption process and be part of your team through to adoption, and maybe beyond. You will meet a number of social workers at various stages of the process, and your working relationship with your social workers and adoption agency is hugely important, so keep this in mind from the first meeting.

You want a constructive and positive relationship, but remember also that this relationship is a *working* relationship. They are *not* your friends. (Though I have several friends who are social workers, I do not work with them, or we have become friends since working together.)

If you are having a bad time or are feeling particularly emotional, talk to your partner or best friend first. I say this from experience, and the experience of others. What you say to a social worker will be noted, recorded in writing and put into your file.

YOUR SOCIAL WORKER

Agencies and LAs each do things differently and use different terms so when you start your journey and have registered with an organisation or agency, I recommend asking them to clarify exactly who you will be working with at which stage so that you can understand the terminology they will use. In general, you will often start by meeting your 'assessing social worker' who will be with you all the way through until you have your child. At that stage, once you have said goodbye to your first social worker, you will work with another who will be your 'post-adoption support social worker'. You may also work with a 'family placements social worker' if your agency has a different person to look after this aspect of the process, or an 'adoption social worker' at the matching stage.

You may experience a number of individual social workers over time in those roles too. If your new social worker is a locum there is a good chance that they will move on. Note too, that all of these social workers share the same offices and know each other, so treat them all with respect. Your child will also have their own social worker whom you will continue to work with after adoption.

We were lucky, we had a good social worker who went the extra mile.

Shanara, adoptive mum

We'll discuss these roles in more detail later in Parts Three and Four of the book, but note now that your adoption team could include any and all of the following:

- Clinical psychologists
- Counselling psychologists
- Attachment psychotherapists
- Educational psychologists
- Social workers and senior social workers
- Occupational therapists
- Mental health workers
- Assistant psychologists
- Specialist support workers
- Link worker
- IRO (Independent Reviewing Officer)

Social care is tough

The reality is that your social worker will have a number of other cases on their books; usually most social workers have more cases than they should and most are skilled at juggling. You will probably want to ask your social worker many questions and I have noticed that sometimes potential adopters hold back on questions because they don't want to appear difficult, tricky or negative. Your social worker, especially an experienced one, will have been asked almost everything you can imagine. If you are like me you will probably think of a question when you're in the bath or lying in bed so I think the best question to ask your new social worker is: 'Is it okay to email you if I have some questions?'.

The truth is that children's social care (the 'umbrella' term for everything including adoption) usually attracts people who care about children and young people, who genuinely want to make a difference. Sadly the system is not set up to always make this ambition possible. It is this that will cause you more stress and anxiety than your adopted child.

They were keen to help us get started and to adopt
Daisy when she was four years old. But when she was
twelve years old and things were beginning to break
down, children's social care were not so helpful. They
only seem to deal with crisis not prevention.

Shola, adoptive mum

Social workers have an extremely difficult job. Social work practice is about making life-changing decisions for children and their families, which often have wider and long-lasting implications for communities and society in general, and the social workers' decision-making is at the heart of the adoption process. They work with children from families who can be particularly disadvantaged by poverty, social trauma, mental health difficulties or learning disabilities. They also have to pay attention to their own ethical choices because social care raises questions about how we support, protect and balance the human rights of parents and children. It is not easy putting children into care, and I have often bitten my tongue when a child has asked why it has taken so long for them to be helped. This also takes me back to my own history and how the social workers viewed my case.

Social workers are under immense pressure, along with the constraints of their department's needs 'to get things done' and meet measured timescales that are not necessarily conducive to creating working relationships with children and adopters. To get the best outcome for your assessment, for example, the social worker needs to sit, talk and slowly get to know you. Good practice is up against bureaucratic needs and a workplace culture that may not necessarily put the child's and your needs first.

Unless you are adopting a baby, you will be adopting a

child or sibling group from the care system and your child's case will probably have gone through the judicial process. Child protection social workers will have supplied evidence to the court that demonstrated that the child's most basic needs were not being met and there may be evidence that the child was abused and/or neglected. This is a strange job and can make social workers feel like a detective. The evidence compiled is there to prevent the child returning to their birth parent(s) because the social worker and their manager feel it is unsafe. Those social workers who have worked in child protection, where their brief was to compile evidence against the birth family, may still work in this way. You may feel that they are trying to 'catch you out', or they may record information about you that is not supportive of your application. I repeat – social workers are not your friends. As potential adopters you will be rightly scrutinised to judge whether you will make good adoptive parents, but there must be safe boundaries in place. You need to decide how much information you will feel comfortable telling your social worker, and be confident that the power for adoption does not rest entirely with the social worker.

Having a 'good' social worker should not be left to luck, we should all expect a good service.

Kate, social worker

What your social worker does and doesn't do
I like to think of the adoption process as a thick, chunky, emotional soup; everything tends to get chucked in the pot. Adopters often assume that they need to tell their social workers everything, that this is the natural order (and the process does lend itself to this 'handing over' of your personal

information). They may ask about your money, your sex lives, your health profile and your families and ex-partners (when you don't even know if they're dead or alive) but it is still vital that your relationship is professional and that you protect your privacy and personal identity. When I was in the assessment process, I was asked numerous questions that I refused to answer. Social workers can be tempted to ask and delve beyond reason and you need to listen to your instincts about what the social worker can and should be asking.

I refused to hand over details of an ex-boyfriend who I lived with for six years in my twenties, and with whom I had no children (not even a pet). There was no need for them to speak to him and I didn't even know where he was. I was also once asked if I had noisy sex and how often and where I had it! I refused to answer the questions as I didn't see what the details of my sex life had to do with looking after a child. I clearly was not Madame Fifi and, to be perfectly honest with you, when you have a new child of any age, sex is not your priority. The need for a good night's sleep becomes your goal. There is also no need for them to see every room in your home or to insist on digging into information that even your close friends or partner don't know.

I am confident and informed so felt comfortable to push back in this relationship, but you may not feel so certain about where the boundaries are. As potential adopters we aim to please; we wish to be liked because we want a child. A good conversation to have with your social worker at the beginning of your relationship is about the types of questions they want to ask you. Take a little time to reflect and think about your responses and what information, both heartfelt and practical, is necessary for the social worker to build a true picture of you and your family.

I also once complained about a social worker who I felt was going beyond the requirements of her role. She was removed and I was given a new social worker who I felt was far more appropriate. I felt very uncomfortable asking for the change in social worker. When we start the adoption journey, we do not want to become known as 'troublemakers', but you need to balance the need to adopt a child against the threat of poor practice. Understanding the process to adoption should enable you to make the best informed decision you can.

Anyone can change their social worker, and anyone can complain. Hopefully you won't need to, but knowing there is a process to do so is important to help you keep the relationship healthy. Nobody should be treated unfairly and all complaints should be treated as a positive opportunity to improve the service.

Mostly though, I have met the most wonderful social workers who go above and beyond the call of duty to get the right placement for the child and the adopter. I think it's important to stress again that many of the social workers you will meet are deeply caring people caught up in a system that has shifted its priorities away from children to an insane amount of bureaucracy and financial directives.

Post-Adoption

Your relationship with your 'post-adoption social worker' will be the most important connection of all. From the start, ensure that you raise any concerns about your child based on your knowledge of them and your instincts. You should have the support in place before you need it, when everything feels OK, instead of waiting until you're fire-fighting and it's too late.

A good working relationship here makes the difference between a potentially problematic set of scenarios around an adoption disruption where you may feel judged as a bad parent or a partnership to help you and your child work through their early life trauma. There will be difficult times ahead, and having a professional partner who you can work with, and discuss options with, is vital.

One of the greatest gifts that you can give yourself is a good relationship with the team, and with other adopters. There are some fantastic organisations and blogs where you can go for support and guidance (see Useful Organisations and Support at the end of the book) and after reading this book I hope you will not feel alone.

CHAPTER 8:

Matching/Family Finding

Match. *Noun. A person or thing that equals or resembles another in some respect. A person or thing able to cope with another as an equal: to meet one's* **match**. *A person or thing that is an exact counterpart of another. A corresponding, suitably associated, or harmonious pair: 'The blue hat and green scarf were not a good* **match**'.

Liberal Dictionary definition

Personally, I think a blue hat and green scarf would work well together – who's to say these colours aren't a 'good match'? I would love to meet the person who wrote that and persuade them otherwise and hopefully broaden their opinion and knowledge.

The 'matching' process is at the heart of the adoption process, and can be a difficult and emotional time, alongside the potential to find your new family member. You will have been through what can be a gruelling assessment period and feel ready to get to the next stage, but remember that there is no requirement that this stage is hurried. Much of the timing is outside your control – depending on which children have been put up for adoption, how old they are and their characteristics. Taking the time to explore all options in a timely manner and working with your social worker and agency to find the best match is absolutely key to the future success and happiness of your adoption – for you and your child. Good matching creates good adoption and good adoption will be successful in allowing the child to catch up on their development – their self-esteem, sense of identity, physical and emotional growth and relationship skills.

You will have been asked to think about what your dreams are for a family. We all have them and our dreams are important – they bring us to the door of adoption. But our dreams and fantasies are part of the early stages of the process. All children and adults are different and a good social worker works with you and the children, recognising you as individuals. If they try to apply a one-size-fits-all approach to your future beautiful family, resist.

Finally, if adoption is your last option and you have exhausted and been exhausted by IVF and all the pain and cost that goes with it, you will be asked – and rightly so – if you have worked through your sadness. As an adoptee I can confirm that it's hard living with feeling second best, or the last resort. You may never say that to your adopted child but they will feel it if you have not come to terms with your loss and grief. The right emotional place to be is excited and fizzy about adopting and welcoming a fully formed young human into your life, whoever they are.

*I think that two years of weekly introspective
psychotherapy is a minimum of necessary preparation
of adopters in order to 'know thyself', which is hugely
expensive and will never happen because everything is
done on the basis of short-term costs.*

*Andrew Wills, academic in Social Work,
University of Plymouth*

HOW MATCHING OCCURS

All parts of the adoption system are geared towards mini-
mising the time between a child coming into care and them
finding a permanent placement. 'Matching' a child and
adopter is not always straightforward or timely, and nor
should it be.

Remember that LA social workers will generally be
knowledgeable about children receiving a care order/
interim care order/placement order – as their team members in child protection will alert the adoption team to
children coming into care for permanent placement or
those being looked-after who are unlikely to return to their
birth family. They will also be aware of new or soon-to-be
approved adopters.

I have seen and heard various approaches to adoption
matching and my least favourite is the use of the formal
matching matrices that do not allow for the unsaid and
unknown and all our complex, beautiful, human emotions.
We cannot be placed into a neat little box. A matrix is used
to assess many aspects of our suitability – for jobs, relationships, holidays and shopping. Computer algorithms predict
what we might like to buy or eat next, and we have all been

on terrible dates with people who look 'perfect' on paper. Matching is not a tick box exercise and the best matching is part intuitive and part pragmatic. The stark reality is that if the match doesn't work, the child will end up back in the system, with a failed placement behind them. Some LAs and agencies still use matrices and similar tools, and every organisation seems to do things differently, which is not at all helpful for the adopters. Personally I think every application needs to feel tailored and handmade for each adopter and child. There are themes that feel and look the same but the dynamics, chemistry and individual personal histories of adopters and children will always be different.

> *We saw a film of our now daughter who was seven years old at the time. We initially wanted a baby or toddler, so when our social worker suggested we looked at her profile we were a little resistant. When we saw her we both fell in love with her and wanted her. She is eleven now and we still can't believe she's ours.*
>
> *Adoptive mum*

ONCE A POSSIBLE LINK IS MADE

If both you and the child's social worker feel you may be a suitable link or match for a child/ren you will be supplied with more information. This will start with the child's background report and profile – their Child Permanence Report (CPR) – which you and your social worker will need to go through with a fine toothcomb, requesting further information if you feel you need to.

Their CPR will detail the health and mental well-being of the child, the birth parents and family. If the child is older it will talk about their interests and achievements. Each report varies according to the history of the child. As children get older they will have experienced more and maybe had a number of foster carers who will have been asked to contribute their knowledge about the child as well as teachers, doctors, etc. It should be enough information to give the adopter a sense of who the child is and what sort of life they have had so far – the bad and the good.

As adopters, you have the opportunity to show yourself to those looking to place a child too. Your profile is your marketing opportunity to sell yourself as the best possible potential adopter for the child that you may be linked with. Some adopters report that they were asked to create a brochure-style document with pictures of the house, garden, child's room and any pets. The link worker looking at a bunch of profiles will want to see something jump out about you that shouts 'we are the new parent(s) for this child'.

Often several potential adopters will be being considered at the same time which is why your own profile must be good. You and your social worker will need to show you in the best possible light. Your profile report is prepared by your social worker, but I suggest that if you are able to get involved with the production of the profile then do so. Profiles can contain films of potential adopters, photographs of their homes, pets and the child/ren's room. Think about how you want to present your home and include lots of well-presented photographs. I remember making sure I had a vase of fresh flowers on my kitchen table – that felt warm and welcoming for me. How would you like the child's room to look? When I spoke to link workers (who help place children) and social workers they said that they looked for authenticity. They liked the personal stories and journeys of adopters and some reported that they were put off by people who presented as *too* perfect – so take note that trying too hard can be detrimental.

In return, you receive the child's profile. Again, each organisation seems to do this differently (it would be great if they shared best practice). Remember that some link profiles will have been made in a hurry and others can be carefully designed to show the child at their best. They will be created by the link worker/child's social worker or perhaps the intern in the office, so look beyond the obvious packaging to the child within.

Sometimes information can be out of date or inaccurate so I recommend pushing your social worker to create a meeting between you and the foster carer if you see a strong profile that you feel could be a match. They will give you the most current and detailed information.

Matching is finding a suitable child from the adopter's point of view and adult from the child's point of view. The child will not always be able to articulate what they want and need, so this will be done for them by their social worker. They will ask if you are what the child needs. You will want to know if they understand what you have to offer. The social worker will be wondering if you understand the significance of the child's current development and what their history means for them and you. They will also be wondering if the child/ren understand the whole process. The child may have attached to their foster carers and all face the knowledge of another loss for the child. Everyone will have sleepless nights!

If you are not selected when you put yourself forwards for a child/ren, it will be a knock, but pick yourself up and keep going. Your match will come along.

Initially we were consciously and unconsciously
looking for a child who looked like us. We saw a photo
of our sons who looked nothing like us but we just
knew they were going to be our children. Now people
say they could not imagine us with any other children.

Adoptive dads

STRUGGLING FOR A MATCH

If you are working with your LA, they may have inhouse children available for adoption. Sometimes there can be large gaps without children being available due to Child Protection teams still processing children's cases with the courts or there may not be any children suitable to be put up for adoption at one time due to their age, trauma and any health issues.

If the local authority has not been able to make a match within three months, or if adopters have been approved for three months or more without a match, adopters will be granted membership of national adoption finding sites (see the list at the back of the book). They can apply to go to an exchange event run by an organisation like Adoption UK or an activity event arranged by CoramBAAF (the successor organisation for the British Association for Adoption and Fostering). The LA or agency may fund this or it could be an additional fee – so it's worth asking about this at the beginning.

You will also be referred to or can ask to be put forward to the Adoption Register (also known as Adoption Match) in England, Wales or Scotland (Northern Ireland has a similar system called ARIS). A lot of children who are not being picked up quickly or locally will be put on these registers, so geography may be a feature of your adoption if you choose this route. Quite a few adopters I spoke to said they joined a site as 'back-up', but you can only access these sites if you have been officially recommended by your adoption organisation, and again, there may be a fee.

There are also other options to discuss with your social worker and explore. Adoption UK's *Children Who Wait* magazine and website contains photos and descriptions of children, and National Adoption Week (generally in October each year) is when organisations hold specific events to help match children and potential adopters.

Child Appreciation Days/Exchange Days are organised by the LAs or agencies at different times of the year, so ask about these. These are events where LAs or agencies can help myth-bust and introduce you to the social workers and other people working with children looking for a permanent home – you'll likely receive information about potential children before the event so that you can discuss them on the day. These are becoming increasingly common and are helpful to learn more about specific children and to present yourself as an adopter; remember they are looking for adopters so they will want to meet you and talk to you.

It doesn't have to be a lottery. Good matching with support and good practice from your social worker, the child's social worker and the independent reviewing officer, all working together, will help create the links needed for you to think about a child or children who could work for you and your family. I cannot stress enough that this is the most important aspect of adoption. If you are prepared and have invested in your own truths and honesty about who you are and how you're going to do adoption with partners, family and dear friends, you will be in an excellent position to get going.

HARDER-TO-PLACE CHILDREN

Older children, children with disabilities and health issues, or children from minority ethnic groups are described as 'harder-to-place' children.

I may need to burst your bubble here, and if so, I apologise. But I need to. The dreams of a beautiful healthy baby to bounce on your knee are unlikely. At various stages of the adoption process, you will be asked to think about and look at older children and children with difficulties if you haven't already considered this option. If you can make the change in your thinking about your expectations and the reality of children being placed for adoption early in the process, you will be in a good place.

We're not so bad – other people's offspring. We're actually rather lovely but feel it deeply every time someone thinks we are what's left on the shelf. I have experienced the negativity around not being the birth child, not looking like my adopted family, not being like them.

There are many children who need a good home and to be loved. I hope that when the links have been made and you receive the child's information you fall in love with their picture and trust me there are a zillion emotions to follow that I can't even begin to explain. I can only say it's huge. I wish I was there with you to hold your hand and make the tea. You must never lose sight of this. It's real and you deserve all the magic that these feelings will bring.

The first thing you should think about is whether you can see yourself with these children who may not fit with your original thoughts about adoption, and may not look like you. I personally still have enough social rebellion left in me to enjoy taking out my blended family with all their individual looks and colours. You may need society to think that your adopted child is your birth child and if you are still stuck in that place you could be missing out on a whole raft of future joy.

If you are considering harder-to-place children you'll probably receive your new ward faster than if you were waiting for a baby or toddler but, just as importantly, the child will have the possibility to find a permanent home more quickly. I beg you to have thought about all aspects of the matching process so that you are ready to go. A child or children need to be linked quickly; they should not be left hanging. If they are left waiting, as they get older they may become more disillusioned because their 'forever family' hasn't shown up – yet. By the time their information does get to the right adopter their behaviour may have deteriorated and their foster placement may have broken down because they feel unwanted. You will be dealing with trauma that could have been prevented.

Matching is about judgement – yours and your support team's. The goal needs to be the best choice that is made collectively with the best information and clear expectations. If at any stage during the matching process you feel a sense of privilege or opportunity due to the process being speeded up I want you to be strong and ask to slow it down again. Matching should not be rushed, it's detailed work. Good matching must be your collective aim otherwise attachment may be tricky, if not unachievable, leading to heartache for all concerned. Matching is not long-stay parking; it's a careful combination of intuition, risk and consideration. To make the best possible choices for the future you need to have collated the best information and done the work and have become a specialist in your field, especially about yourself.

The recent push to speed up the adoption process adds new limits on the time a social worker can spend with you and your case. I beg you to not let that impact on the matching and that's why I have written this chapter to encourage and prepare you to be the best match for the right child. When I started my art career I began with a Foundation Course; it was a diagnostic programme that allowed the students to explore all the elements of visual art. We started with drawing and then took turns on a carousel of skills, techniques, concepts and experiments. By experiencing a diagnostic process we moved towards our strengths but learned about other subjects along the way which broadened our understanding as we chose our specialism. I feel that matching is like this. We congregate in the area of adoption bringing with us our own lives, experiences and ideas. We will recognise and be drawn towards different things while we glean information and ideas from others. There will be mistakes, as there is in art, but sometimes those mistakes can become the most interesting and important aspect of our work.

In with all this, it is important that you feel no pressure from the professionals or from yourself. To reject a child at matching stage is not a failure if you are not convinced that the child is right for you, and vice versa, after you have factored in the unknown. You may be worried that the door will close and you will not find another child but there will always be children needing a permanent, safe, loving home. Intuition coupled with good research and information needs to be your mantra – you will find your child.

PART THREE

Bringing Your Child Home

CHAPTER 9:

Financial and Legal Support

Before we talk about how to enjoy a successful first few months with your child, I want to look at the financial and other support you may be able to access. Arming yourself with as much information as possible is empowering and the way to ensure the financial and professional help that you and your child may need.

After the adoption, you are not left unsupported. Your post-adoption social worker will keep in close contact, as will your child's social worker. If you adopted through an agency, they will be in regular contact with you after the adoption (agencies tend to be more open about their post-adoption support so you will know the structure of what is offered in this case).

Financial support options will vary between England, Wales, Scotland and Northern Ireland and in each LA, so do your research through your local government website and talk to your post-adoption social worker to ensure that you know how to access the options I will discuss, plus whether or not they may affect your own rights to receiving benefits.

Looking at your local council website and talking to your social worker is a good start for those new parents who want to understand what is available. By this time, you will undoubtedly be a master at complicated forms and application procedures, so prepare yourselves for another round of assembling paperwork in order to secure your entitlement and understand your rights as early as possible – it's helpful to have this underway and your questions answered before your matching process is completed.

In this chapter, I'll cover the basics of:

- Statutory adoption pay and leave (the 'statutory' rights of an adoptive payment to financial support from the state for 52 weeks post-adoption)
- Settling-in grant – money which can be applied for to cover new items needed for your child such as a cot or bed, etc.
- Child benefit/tax credits
- Disability benefits/carer's allowance
- Adoption support from your LA (including the Adoption Allowance – regular money paid weekly/monthly to an adopter following placement, determined by potential extra needs of the child – the sum is means-tested and follows an assessment from the LA)
- Adoption Support Fund.

STATUTORY ADOPTION PAY AND LEAVE

When you adopt a child you may be eligible for Statutory Adoption Leave and Pay ('statutory' meaning that this is the legal minimum). The government supports many newly adoptive parents through the state system, in a similar way to maternity/paternity pay and leave regulations.

Pay

Adoption pay is paid for a total of 39 weeks (the same as maternity pay) to one parent of a newly adopted child. For the first six weeks you will get 90 per cent of your average weekly earnings. Over the remaining 33 weeks you'll receive the lower sum of either Statutory Adoption Pay (currently £151.20 a week) or 90 per cent of your average weekly earnings. Some of this time may be needed in the weeks prior to your child coming to live with you as you spend lots of time with them at their foster home.

You should be eligible for adoption pay if you meet the following criteria:

- You have been continuously employed by your employer for at least 26 weeks
- You earn at least £120 a week (before tax), and have done so for at least eight weeks before the week you are matched with a child.

Also, the same eligibility rules apply as the adoption leave.

Leave

Adoption leave is up to 52 weeks, broken down into 26 weeks of 'Ordinary Leave' and 26 weeks of 'Additional Leave'. Only one person can take this leave (the other partner could get paternity leave or 'Shared Parental Leave' which is discussed on page 116). If you're wondering about the difference between the two types, 'Ordinary Leave' is generally seen as standard/usual, and 'Additional Leave' is an option that you may or may not take. Note that your employment rights are slightly different if you take Additional Leave, in that your job is protected more strongly by the law during the Ordinary Leave period. Ensure that you read up on this and that you check your employment contract carefully.

To be eligible for adoption leave you must be an 'employee' and provide the correct notice and proof. Within seven days of being matched with a child you must tell your employer the following:

- How much leave you want
- The start date of your leave
- The date the child is due to be placed with you.

Your leave can generally be taken from up to two weeks before your child moves in with you, from the date that your baby is born (in surrogacy cases) or within 28 days of your child arriving in the country (if adopting from abroad). Your employer may ask for this in writing and ask for proof and they must then confirm your leave start and end dates within 28 days.

If you are entitled to adoption leave, you can also claim paid 'time off work' to attend five adoption appointments after you have been matched with a child.

Shared Parental Leave and Statutory Shared Parental Pay

If you wish, you can share up to 50 weeks of adoption leave with Shared Parental Leave (SPL) and up to 37 weeks of pay through Statutory Shared Parental Pay (SSPP). This leave is fairly flexible – you can take it all in one go, or take it in blocks of time (up to three separate blocks) separated by periods of work. You can choose to be on leave together or take it in turns to do so.

To be eligible each of you must:

- Have worked for the same employer continuously for at least 26 weeks by the time you are matched with a child
- Continue with that employer while you take the leave
- Be employees not 'workers' (so not self-employed or on temporary contracts)
- Each earn on average £120 or more each week (before tax)
- Give your employer at least eight weeks of written notice of your leave dates.

If you both want to share the parental leave and pay, if either of you is a 'worker' rather than an employee you can share the parental pay but not the leave. If one of you earns less than £120 a week, you can share the parental leave but not the pay.

Shared Parental Pay

If you are eligible for parental leave, you can end the adoption leave and pay early, and can then take the rest of the 52 weeks as Shared Parental Leave and the rest of the 39 weeks as shared parental pay.

Statutory Shared Parental Pay is paid at the same rate as adoption pay or 90 per cent of your weekly earnings, whichever is lower, though, the first six weeks is different. Adoption pay for the first six weeks is 90 per cent of your salary whereas the shared parental pay is a flat amount per week.

Workers/employees: Your employer can tell you if you are a worker or an employee. As an employee you have extra employment rights and responsibilities that don't apply to workers who aren't employees (which you will find in your employment contract).

Self-Employed

Unfortunately, if you are self-employed there is currently no entitlement to any adoption pay, which I feel is outrageous. State maternity benefits for the self-employed exist, however, there is no equivalent benefit for self-employed adopters. The Independent Review, led by renowned entrepreneur Julie Deane OBE, is currently advocating for adoptive self-employed parents to have the same level of support as self-employed birth parents.

SETTLING-IN GRANT

Ask your social worker for information about how to apply for this one-off payment, for which some parents are eligible. It is usually claimed to pay for larger items such as beds, car seats or prams for when your child arrives, but I find in reality that it is rarely granted.

CHILD BENEFIT/TAX CREDITS

Generally, as soon as your child comes to live with you, you are able to start claiming basic rights such as child benefit plus free school meals, and free NHS prescriptions, dental and optical care for your child (often from the Monday subsequent to moving in).

In England, child benefit is currently £21.05 per week for your eldest first child and £13.95 for all subsequent children; it is paid every four weeks. Some of the money will have to be repaid through the tax system if the person claiming or their legal partner earns £50,000 or more per year.

If you are receiving universal tax credits, you should be able to receive an additional child payment if you adopt. Do talk to your social worker or benefits office for details of how to apply.

DISABILITY BENEFITS/CARER'S ALLOWANCE

Disability living allowance (DLA) is paid (to an adult) for children under 16 who qualifies as having caring or mobility needs due to disability/ill health. This should be discussed when a child moves to your home so that you can begin the paperwork to become the child's 'appointee' for the payments and have the records transferred with the DWP. Children over 16 will claim the Personal Independence Payment (PIP) themselves directly.

A carer's allowance is possible for one designated person caring for a child receiving the DLA or PIP in certain circumstances.

ADOPTION SUPPORT FROM YOUR LA

We've discussed the EHCP/HCP earlier and that is often part of the adoption process. This allows for an assessment through your LA to determine whether your child will require support with their educational, social or care needs going forwards – be it speech therapy, counselling, play therapy, physiotherapy, etc. You are entitled to this assessment by your LA as to the post-adoption support you may need for your child – and this can be requested at any point prior or post the adoption order.

Ensure that you are on top of this and have everything you wish in writing as you complete the adoption process. Discussing necessary help should be part of the conversation when the link has been made, and the child's Child Permanence Report is reviewed. Getting discussions around your child's needs on the record will be important for when the child has settled and new revelations or developments occur. It will be so much harder to access support and funding once the adoption is legal. The EHCP/HCP will take into account the child's history and current or prospective needs, and should be part of the process even without any identifiable significant development issues purely as a precaution to identify development issues early (early interventions). Everyone around the child needs to be included in contributing to the support package; it will speed things up and broaden the scope. Sharing knowledge, information and costing is crucial for making this work well.

I recommend that as you are getting to know the child and discussing them with their foster parent/s and support team, you gather evidence that demonstrates whether your child has special needs and if you suspect your child needs additional support, now or in the future. Adopters can work with their adoption social worker to visit a GP to make a recommendation for further assessment that will be included in the court hearing or acknowledged for post-adoption support.

Of course, sometimes situations change and unseen problems may arise or needs may change after the adoption has been finalised. Much post-adoption support is required too when the children reach teenage years with all the hormones and fireworks that arrive. Any assessments prior to the adoption, and for up to three years after the adoption, will be made by the LA responsible for the adoption/your child's local authority (the 'placement authority'). Should you require a reassessment or a new assessment of your child's needs after three years post-adoption, the LA for the adoptive family's address will be the responsible authority. Knowing where you need to go with requests is important.

If at any point you require a reassessment of the post-adoption support or a new assessment (perhaps most practical for those who adopt prior to the child going into the education system), then know that you can apply/approach the LA by:

- Visiting your GP to prompt an assessment
- Working with your child's school to instigate an assessment or reassessment
- Directly approaching the LA with your concerns.

Once the LA has created a draft assessment report you should be invited to read it and make comments/amendments, and I recommend that you go through it very carefully.

Drafting your bid for funding (whether through the EHC or Adoption Support Fund, as below) needs to be as thorough as possible, and the language needs to be bolted down by you and the other professionals who all have experience of working with LAs. I cannot stress enough how important it is that you do this work when life is calm, yet keeping your child's worst day in mind when you write it.

LAs can use what I call 'white noise language' and be deliberately vague. This means they could potentially wriggle out of funding something further down the line, so pin specifics down and watch the wording. For example, if you insist that your child needs speech therapy, then 'child would benefit from speech therapy' will be hard to enforce but if you amend the language to 'child must have a weekly

30-minute one-to-one speech therapy session until no longer required', it is harder for them to wriggle out of funding.

Unfortunately, although the LA is bound by law in terms of providing an assessment if requested, there is no legal requirement compelling them to provide any support recommended by the assessment. The LA will decide what provisions to offer in terms of post-adoption services depending on the needs of your child – for example, extra parenting skills courses, therapies or respite options. Any support can be commissioned by them and provided by a third party or separate adoption support agency such as the Adoption UK Family Support Service, the adoption agency, the NHS (and through them CAMHS for mental health support) or an independent provider.

Education, Health And Care Plan (EHCP)

Your child's EHCP/HCP is often part of agreeing adoption terms (and I talk about this in more detail in the next chapter). The EHCP sets out the provisions/plan to meet the special education needs (SEN) of the child or young person in order to allow them to reach their full potential across their education, health and social care. The plan is for children and young people aged up to 25 years who need more support than is available through general special educational needs support.

The plan should enable improved outcomes by having the child and family at the heart of what happens, by enabling collaborative partnerships across education, health and care as well as with the community voluntary sector, parents and young people. The plan needs to cover all aspects of your child's communication and interaction; cognition and learning; behaviour, emotional and social development; sensory and physical needs and medical condition.

It should be a collaborative project between you and the

school, plus any input from other professionals who can supply diagnosis, evidence and ideas. Central government delegates the funds to local authorities which then by law have to assess your application. I cannot stress enough how important it is to write this document with the professional team that is around your child. It is a tough one to do alone and may be more likely rejected.

You will need to see your GP to get referrals for psychologists and other professionals to assess your child's needs. This can take months, so start early. It's all about gathering evidence that demonstrates your child has special needs and that additional support is needed. Once your LA has created their draft report you should be invited to read it and make amendments.

The EHCP/HCP plan should also have a section that includes the best choice of school for your child's needs. The school needs to be named and the choice should be justified. (If you are hoping that your child can be funded to go to a private school then expect a battle; many adopters fund this themselves if they can afford it.)

Adoption Allowance

The purpose of the Adoption Allowance is to provide a regular payment to facilitate the adoption of children who might otherwise not be adopted due to the likely extra costs needed for specialist support or care, according to the Children and Families Act 2014.

The payment/s is determined by the LA looking after the child before the adoption and this scheme makes regular allowance payments ('personal budgets') to adopters under specific circumstances – for example, if a child needs specific additional support due to illness, disability, or emotional or behavioural difficulties causing extra expense. The personal budget is a sum of money made available to secure specific adoption support services, through either 'direct payments' to the family so that they can purchase services themselves or the LA spends on the family's behalf, or even a combination of both. The amount of money offered will vary, as this allowance is means-tested so the local authority will take into account the financial resources of the family.

A personal budget can only be set in place following the assessment. The assessment reviews the child's short- and long-term needs and it will take into account your current financial resources and the amount required in respect of reasonable outgoings and the financial needs and resources of the child. If a decision is made that regular payments should be made, it will then be decided what the frequency of these payments will be and the amount of the financial support (to be reviewed annually).

The benefit of securing direct payments is that it gives greater flexibility over how additional support is arranged, as long as you are spending your personal budget on the support that meets your agreed assessment with the local authority.

Once you start receiving payments, you must keep a detailed record of how you are using the money and retain all paperwork and receipts as the LA will likely ask for information as to how the direct payments have been spent (and can ask for the monies to be repaid if necessary).

If your assessment has stated that you are able to pay for respite care or for additional assistance of your choice, it can sometimes be possible to use someone you already know, such as a family member, but you cannot use direct payments to pay a close relative who lives in the same household as you (unless in exceptional circumstances). So this doesn't prevent you from using close relatives living elsewhere, as long as the local authority agree that this family member will meet the needs of the child. (The rules for employing family members varies slightly depending on where you live in the UK, so check with your local authority.)

Also, be aware that if you are paying a family member or friend directly, then you could be taking on the responsibilities of an employer, unless they are self-employed, so explore this option further in terms of their tax requirements before you take on this responsibility.

If the local authority does not accept that your child needs support, it will not offer direct payments. You can challenge the decision if you wish, via their complaint's procedure (or the Local Government Ombudsman). Most parents I know who have succeeded in receiving direct payments have had to challenge an initial refusal. Given the potential breadth of this option, and the flexibility it offers, this is the best way to secure funding for your family needs.

Adoption Support Fund (ASF)

This fund was set up in 2015 to provide funding for therapeutic support to adoptive families across England, Wales, Scotland and Ireland via the Department for Education, as historically families have struggled to get help in this area. It invested almost £200 million in about 50,000 families in the first five years and is currently set to run until July 2021, and its future after that is still to be announced.

To access this fund, your local authority first needs to carry out the assessment of your family's adoption support needs. The application is then made by the LA within three months of the assessment where the assessment has identified that therapeutic services will benefit the family. If successful, the money is released to the LA and it will communicate with you about your choice of provider and service. I recommend that you discuss the types of services and providers available with your social worker. (Again, these services can be made available through the LA, independent or NHS providers or CAMHS).

In terms of the amount available, the ASF will give up to a maximum amount per child of £5,000 for therapy, plus an additional potential sum of £2,500 for each child if supplemental specialist assessment is required. (Therapy and assessment above these amounts and up to a limit of £30,000 requires match funding by the local authority).

Take a look at the full gamut of what is available through the fund online (details are at the end of the book). In general the fund aims to provide therapies that enhance the child's relationship with learning or their school environment, improve emotional regulation and manage behaviour, and improve their ability to access a positive family life and social relationships (it doesn't cover specific assessment requirements such as assessing for ADHD, autism, etc.).

Examples of the therapies funded are:

- Improving relationships with friends, family, teachers
- Improving learning
- Improving emotional and behavioural development
- Improving confidence.

Therapeutic support

When I tried to get a national view of funding for adopted children, I learned that there is help but – frustratingly – each region does it differently. In Kent, for example, it is called IASK (Information and Advice Support Kent) and in Devon it is DIAS (Devon Information and Support), so my advice would be to research online for what is available and how to apply. (There is more information at the end of the book.)

I sometimes feel that funding bids require the experience of a professional funding bid writer! Regular people like me may not have these skills or understand the tricks of the trade; again this part of the process forces an expectation that we all have the same skillset as those designing the application. It can feel tortuous applying for funding and it relies upon local arrangements.

If you have adopted your child through an agency, it may be better placed to take on the application or may be enlightened and supportive enough to have its own packages in place because it recognises that children require different support at different times in their lives. Generally support comes under psychological/counselling services, which is accessed through the health route not the social services route (unless there are significant issues under Section 47 or Section 17, Children Act 1989). Again, know the law and refer to your copy of the Children Act 1989.

The first hurdle is to find a GP who may understand the issue. She/he may prescribe medication, which you could struggle with, depending on your views of pharmaceutical interventions over a range of other therapies. The first solutions you could discuss with your GP include the following:

- Talking therapies
- Family therapy
- Play therapy
- Creative arts therapy
- Drama therapy
- Therapeutic life story work/narrative therapy

- Psychotherapy
- Therapeutic parenting.

Being prescribed medication is, unfortunately, a goal for many parents. Helping and supporting a child who has experienced trauma will be hard work without medication and requires extreme determination and consistency, as well as patience. You don't want medication to be the first option for your child if there are other options.

These different therapy models support children (and their caregivers) where there has been trauma, and chronic symptoms resulting from such. Not all types of therapy will be appropriate or helpful in every case, but discussions with your GP will help you to identify the best support to aid your child.

Many GPs prioritise Cognitive Behaviour Therapy (CBT) as a form of trauma therapy, and I have looked after children with trauma who benefited greatly from CBT. For me, using creativity – through art therapy (in which I'm a trained professional) and narrative therapy, for example – have been the most effective with ALL of my children. This enables and encourages the children and young people to express themselves because often, when you strip all the anxiety and anger away, what's left is an unheard, unloved voice.

You may need to try more than one, as some children click better with certain approaches and the individual delivering them, and be prepared to travel to find the right therapist and therapy for your child's needs (especially if you live in a rural area).

CYPMHS/CAMHS

If the GP believes that your child warrants further therapeutic support, their first step will be to refer her/him to CYPMHS

(Children and Young People's Mental Health Service), often referred to under its previous local name of CAMHS (Children and Adolescent Mental Health Services).

Sadly this is one of the children's health services that has suffered outrageously due to cuts. CYPMHS is organised locally and these NHS-funded provisions will encompass numerous statutory, voluntary and school-based services which vary greatly due to local decisions on priorities, again down to awareness and understanding.

The GP will most likely only steer you towards CYPMHS if the consultation suggests that your child is in a bad way (which can be frustrating because when I've taken children and young people to the doctor they usually sit politely and quietly and don't really answer the questions from the complete stranger honestly). With waiting lists for CYPMHS support so long, many adopters seek their own non-medication therapies. Most CYPMHS will have a long referral time of up to 12 months or more (I have heard of a three year wait) by which time your child may have hit a crisis. Their negative behaviour is allowed to become hard-wired. There are exceptions for emergencies, but attempted suicide should not need to be a trigger to be bumped up the list – factoring prevention into its planning should be viewed as a good cost-saving device.

CYPMHS will triage referral. Depending on which region your CYPMHS service is in, it may just offer an advisory service such as attending meetings or observing your child play. The CYPMHS appointment will often have your child see a child psychologist after which there will most likely be a referral to see a specialist who will undertake a structured assessment which will then be referred to their CYPMHS team for a potential diagnosis. Once you eventually get through this process you are likely to receive some time-limited intervention. Most work with children is fixed at six weeks, following the NHS model. In reality, of course, six weeks is about the time it takes for your child to reach a level of trust in order to begin to reveal themselves in whatever way works for them.

If, at any time, the referral fails, it all goes back to 'square one', i.e. the GP. By referrals failing, I mean that you and the child have not been successful in demonstrating how serious the issues are. Bear in mind that benchmarking is a moveable feast according to budgets available. I have been very clearly told – and I now pass on to others – 'Keep going, keep asking'.

You, as the adopted parent, along with the social worker and school, can devise a support package – with or without talking therapies – that works just for your child. If I am honest, I would advise every adoptive parent to go straight to alternative therapies that are creative because they work for children (who are not best suited to talking therapies) and young people and can be a fantastic resource while you are waiting or exploring diagnosis and CAMHS options. The results are staggering and the professionals know this. It is the funding that is the problem.

The skills an adopter needs to get through this is persistence in making continuous and assertive demands, and being able to judge the appropriateness of the advice and suggested interventions at every stage of events.

Andrew Wills, academic in Social Work,
University of Plymouth

CHAPTER 10:

Working with Your Child's School

Sadly children who have experienced trauma tend to have a more challenging time at school, often because of experiences at critical times in their development. I have distinct memories of not being able to concentrate and my attitude to learning was affected by the fear and threats coming from my home life.

If your child is coming out of the area you will need to find a school that you feel will understand and cater for your child's needs. If your child is already at a school in your area and is happy there it makes sense for them to stay, even if it requires a longer drive or other transport to get them there. You need to give the school time to see if it's working for your child. If you are a new parent, it can feel daunting trying to understand the complexities of the national curriculum, behaviour policy and so much more. Education is another whole new language (with yet more acronyms) to get your head around alongside children's social care and adoption. (I struggled to grasp everything and wanted to know how decisions are made so became a school governor, which I thoroughly recommend.) It will also take a while for the new parent/s, particularly of an older child, to understand the child's feelings and relationship with their school, and the dynamics between friends and teachers.

If siblings attend the same school and have a tricky relationship, one of them may benefit from being moved. I spoke with several adoptive parents where siblings had been competitive and argumentative and the separation of the school day enabled the children to experience a new relationship with each other, allowing them to talk about their experiences of school in their own way, without the conflict. The adopted parents I spoke with said it was transforming and another mum said, 'I don't know why we didn't think of doing this earlier'.

Personally, I would not choose to change a child's school soon after the adoption unless they pathologically hate it. Remember, the relationship you have with the school is deeply important and worth investing in; most staff and teachers are sensible and kind and will bend to work with you and your child. Again, much power lies with being fully aware of your and your child's rights – and what responsibility lies with the school.

YOUR SCHOOL TEAM

When your child moves in, whether they are at their old school or starting a new one, the school needs to sit down with you and your child. Ensure that the school is aware of at least the outlines of your child's pre-adoption history.

The key people in your school who you need to know and to ensure that you have access to are:

- Their class teachers
- The teaching assistants (TAs), Learning Support Assistants (LSAs) and Emotional Learning Support team Assistants (ELSAs)
- Learning Mentors
- Special Educational Needs Coordinator (SENCo)
- Heads of Year/Form Tutors/Heads of House
- School Pastoral Team

Every looked-after child will already have a Personal Education Plan (PEP) – including educational strengths and weaknesses plus educational objectives. A PEP meeting would have been held every term with the child, their social worker (and possibly the Independent Reviewing Officer (IRO)), foster carer, SENCo and one or more teachers (usually the class teacher or head/deputy head) associated with the child. The details of what is held in the PEP will vary from one LA to another, and will travel with the child if there is a change of school.

You must try to understand the position of the schools as many are under financial pressures, performance targets and so on. The teachers with the experience and passion for our young people's education know how the system works; they understand the flaws within it, and they can be great allies. It's all about relationships, partnership and working together. And when you need to, being able to stamp your feet a little.

In your child's school there will be someone who can be their 'key' adult or 'designated teacher', someone who is either brought in or already working there who will make themselves available for your child, and that means consistently saying hello and goodbye, and asking how are you? – someone who behaves like nothing seems too much trouble for your child. This adult can keep an eye and ear out for your child, observe their friendships and report back to you if needed.

Children who have come into the care system have experiences of distress and trauma which can affect their behaviour, especially in group settings. I cannot stress enough just how often you and your child's teachers need to put themselves in the shoes of your child and imagine how they must be feeling. If strategies are not in place to enable them to cope then learning opportunities are lost and children can be labelled, seen as being withdrawn or having difficult and challenging behaviour. Your child has the right to the same educational experience as other children but it's an art to find the balance between what we hope and want for them alongside what they can manage, given everything else that's going on.

Creative thinking is the root of our love and support for our adopted children. If they're struggling, don't give up. Children who have experienced trauma learn differently, but these behaviours and instincts need to be welcomed and seen as another way of working, not a challenge or problem. Use positive language and if you don't hear it, ask for it. By changing the language we can change attitudes.

Talk to the headteacher or the CEO of the Academy Trust or the arrangement for school clusters in your area. Remember there are fewer opportunities for future chances for our children if they have a bad educational experience. Access courses and further education used to enable a 'second chance' for those who fall out of the education system but, like many educational opportunities, these have been cut away so it is even more important to do whatever it takes to build an effective relationship with the school.

YOUR EDUCATION, HEALTH AND CARE PLAN (EHCP)

If you feel that your child needs extra support at school your EHCP is your first route to making that happen. This legally binding document protects your child's funding and its direction up to the age of 25 (but does not cover university education). From your child benefiting from attending a different school to receiving one-to-one support in the classroom or art therapy to improve emotional strength, this is the document that should secure the options and funding for these needs.

The process can be started by you, your child's school or your child if over 16, by requesting the forms from the relevant LA. Working with the school is the best way to be successful because they will have knowledge and experience in creating these, plus they know the likely needs of your child. The school will also have the PEP which feeds into most of the educational aspects of your child's personal EHCP/HCP, so they will be able to fully support this part of the process. If the school does not support your belief that your child requires extra support, then do begin the process yourself.

If your application is unsuccessful you can appeal and the good news is that many of those who appeal an initial rejection are successful. Remember that the LA will be trying to protect its budgets, but you can require an EHCP assessment for any child if you simply: a) suspect that the child has special needs, and b) suspect that extra support is needed for them in the education environment. It can feel like jumping through more hoops because they do not make this easy for us – but here are my top tips. Your application should be:

- Clear, concise, understandable, accessible, forward-looking and outcomes focused.
- Don't forget to detail your required outcomes in a SMART manner – they should be specific, measurable, attainable, realistic and time bound.
- Do an online search for 'sample EHCP' to find a template to use, and always overwrite rather than underwrite when providing supporting details. (I adapted the online form because the LA is looking for full and informative comments and the boxes are never big enough.)

The main areas to consider are:

- Cognition and learning (work with your child's teacher on this)
- Communication and interaction (talk to other professionals to get a rounded response)
- Social, emotional and mental health (again, work with your school on this area)
- Self-care and independence (this is very important to consider)
- Health: physical and mental (including consultations, physical development and hopes for the future)
- What helps us as a family (add this if it isn't on your own LA's form as it is a useful opportunity to reflect and challenge what is available).

Again, the school will be part of the child's PEP and much of the information you need for this application will be in there. Choose your language carefully in order to be measured but also fully honest about the behaviour on your child's worst day to get what you need from the system.

The other route to getting extra support for your child is through the school's SENCo lead. This will rely on their understanding, knowledge and persistence in accessing services which may be 'privately' purchased by the school or the multi-school academy trust (MAT) of which the school is a part. You are perfectly entitled to politely question the school's policies and values and suggest ideas. Sometimes teachers just don't know about the latest sensory therapy or wriggle seat, so share your knowledge and aim to work in partnership.

PUPIL PREMIUM

The Pupil Premium provides extra funding to state schools to allow for supplemental support to disadvantaged pupils including, but not restricted to, all children adopted from care (or who have left care under an adoption order, Special Guardianship Order or Residence Order in England and Wales). Children of families receiving certain benefits (often those in receipt of free school meals), and children of forces' families from reception class through to Year 11 are also included.

Currently up to £2,345 per pupil per school year is available for every adopted child, with the intention that the school can invest in specific support measures to boost their education and address the issues that may be preventing the child from reaching their potential.

BULLYING

Bullying is insidious and hurtful and can cost lives. It happens every day in our schools, and is even tougher for adopted and fostered children as they usually have a less secure base. Even if you have adopted your child as a baby, there is already history that will have some impact on the child's feelings of loss and rejection in the future. I was cruelly bullied at school by a group of 'popular mean girls' who no doubt had their own issues. I was targeted because my way of coping with the chaos and abuse in my adopted home was to withdraw and be quiet, and this made me easy prey.

Bullying takes many forms, from verbal teasing, name calling and mimicking to social exclusion, peer pressure and social media/technology harassment. Broadly speaking, girls choose to enact more emotional and subtle forms of abuse, such as gossip and exclusion, while for boys, physical violence could be involved.

Adopted children may have experienced a number of these behaviours from their birth family, and those who feel isolated, anxious and have low self-esteem sadly often struggle to reach out and tell their parents or teacher what is going on. Their experience of chaotic relationships and poor boundaries, combined with a shifting emotional age, can cause internal conflict when trying to respond to bullying which is, after all, abuse. This can lead to behaviour at home and school being misinterpreted and misdiagnosed, so keep a sharp eye on your child and how they describe their school days and look for unexplained changes of behaviour and signs of social difficulties.

It is often wise to begin with a discreet word with the school. This is when good relationships with your SENCo, pastoral care team and headteacher/deputy head or those responsible for school-wide pastoral care are helpful. They will be able to make subtle observations and begin work to ensure that your child feels safe to learn – children can't engage with school if they don't feel safe. Be aware of the school policy for dealing with bullying and ensure that it is followed. You need to be clever and calm – easier said than done, I know.

If you learn that your child is bullying another, take time to digest this difficult information. Imagine what feelings and emotions bullying another child is giving to your child: perhaps a sense of power, popularity or confidence? These are feelings around self-esteem and demonstrate that your child may need more opportunity to experience these feelings in a safe and kind way. If your child is a bystander, they will be suffering from conflicting feelings of popularity, shame and guilt. They need activities and support that do not add to their shame but will offer opportunities to feel different and empowered to feel positive about doing the right thing.

> *Don't be frightened to ask, ask and ask again and, if*
> *you still don't get what you need, ask again.*
> *Samantha Davidson, Deputy Head Teacher*

I think it's important for teachers and parents to recognise that adopted children will have issues around identity. Can you imagine being removed from your birth family, changing your name, and having to learn the culture and history of your new family (bearing in mind you probably do not resemble them)? You are going to need some outlet for experimenting with your own identity. When I was at secondary school I discovered Punk and overnight transformed myself from a quiet, natural-haired, bored student into a spectacle of self-expression. Some children may express this in moderation, some like myself with an artistic flare may be more determined and visual. Allow your child some choices of non-conformity. If we and our schools are too rigid and deny a traumatised child the opportunity to express themselves I cannot see much opportunity to reach them and release that child's potential.

I recall only one switched-on teacher who went out of her way to meet my needs and make allowances for my behaviour, as caused by trauma. In the 1970s, our awareness of the effects of trauma were nowhere near as advanced as it is today. I was lucky to find a school that encouraged its staff to be intuitive and creative, so I was allowed and encouraged to draw and paint. I felt comfort and calmness in these activities and my teacher's encouragement and kindness stays with me today. Thank you, Ms Nixon.

CHAPTER 11:

Your Social Worker, GP, Dentist and Optician

Your child will need you to access the post-adoption health-care they need. Working with your post-adoption social worker may feel like a long way off right now, but this relationship will come round faster than you expect.

Your post-adoption social worker has several roles within her or his organisation, whether that is a local authority or agency. They are there to help you and your child if you need them. They will usually run or be part of a family support group. It's also part of their job to work with you to identify and activate therapeutic support for you and your child. I have met and heard through the adopters I spoke to that a good one is wonderful; they can smooth the way for ideas and projects. They are there to help you ask for support.

Though this is potentially a wonderful relationship, remember that it is still a professional association. However, embrace your post-adoption social worker as a useful first contact for teething issues after your child moves in. They will also be an invaluable guide to accessing wider resources and a greater understanding of how the systems work.

HIDDEN HEALTH ISSUES

Adopted children share the same health risks and problems as their peers, but often to a greater degree, and in the context of obstacles such as discord within their own families, frequent changes of home or school, and lack of access to the support and advice of trusted adults. Their health issues are largely due to poverty, poor parenting, chaotic lifestyles and abuse or neglect. Also a large number of children from the care system have mental health issues, which could include anxiety, depression and hyperactivity.

In my experience every child who has come into my care has had a least one physical health issue. These are usually eyes and sight issues, dental issues, speech and language, bedwetting and soiling, difficulty with physical coordination or asthma and eczema. Always take a new child to see their GP, a dentist and an optician. It's a good way to find out what issues have been reported before and if there are any patterns in their health.

If you are new to parenting you will soon learn how a child's aches and pains and other symptoms usually have a simple and practical solution. A little boy I know, who was adopted at five after several years in foster care, was from the beginning of his placement worrying his adopted parents. He would sit rocking, holding his face while mumbling to himself. The little boy came from Eastern European heritage and his adopted parents' imaginations were travelling all over the place. It took a trip to the GP to put an end to all their fears and speculation; sadly the little boy's time in foster care had meant that he had not had any dental appointments. His teeth were rotten, another physical identification of neglect. A visit to a dentist followed, then a referral to the hospital to have six of his teeth removed, and the doctor prescribed antibiotics to clear up the infection. Within a few days the adopters saw a transformation and learned a big lesson: avoid speculation and look at your adopted child's actual health.

I also should say that it is quite common for children who have not received the nurture and care that they needed when younger to use pain – real or not – to get your sympathy and attention. It's tricky, they obviously require you to notice and comfort them, but at the same time you don't want this behaviour to become a thing. Every child I have looked after in my home has done this, even at 18 years old. I have to gauge the child and let them have some fuss and attention to start with then I reduce it down to the same levels that my secure birth children, who rarely complain of pain or hurts, receive. The worst thing you can do is help make your child a hypochondriac. After caring for so many children now, I have become the person who says, 'You're going to school even if you're on a stretcher'.

Like social workers, teachers, the police and all the other professionals around the child, GPs are very busy, but I have never met one to date who has not taken seriously the health and well-being of an adopted child. I have found that a visit to my GP tends to stimulate the actions required for a good EHCP or other route to therapeutic support, so foster that relationship well.

CHAPTER 12:

Your Relationship with the Birth Family

Contact with the birth family is often termed 'family time' (a term which I find counter-intuitive). The aim is to facilitate a healthy relationship between the child and the birth family, while still keeping the child firmly embedded in the stable adoptive environment.

The majority of adoptive families have contact arrangements with their child's birth parents or some relative or birth sibling; this is often indirect (such as private 'letterbox contact', which is perhaps a yearly exchange of written information via the agency), but contact of some type. Advice here is difficult as every child's situation will be different, and their reactions to and ways of dealing with the connection will vary according to age, emotional connection and past history. Once a child is adopted, the adoptive family will usually control the decisions made about ongoing contact and this should be done with the welfare and the best interests of the child first. There is often a disconnection between recommendations, agreed contact and what actually happens, so I gently suggest that you begin the adoption with a healthy respect and positive mindset about an ongoing relationship with the birth family in a safe and supported way and see how it goes. Talk to your social worker about any concerns and issues and they will be able to offer advice relevant to your specific circumstances.

Some adopters have reported that a phased-out direct contact worked well as it gave the child closure, then contact could become indirect (letterbox) only. The adopted parent is the overall organiser and enabler of contact, so in my view, will know the child better than anyone and needs to make caring decisions for the child.

The most important thing for adopters to confidently grasp is that they should take their time when the placement starts just getting to know their child. There is no legal obligation for the adoptive families to maintain contact with the birth families after the adoption order; contact arrangements may or may not be part of the order, or a voluntary agreement may be discussed.

Adopters must not be pressured by the birth family or social workers into contact without full understanding of what that entails and what will be said to the child. A child adopted as a baby will have differing needs than a teenager with extended birth family relationships, but the adoption system welcomes the changes that now recognise a child's need to understand where they have come from and what this means for their identity. The adoption agency will recognise that contact is part of this development, along with potential therapy and life story work (see Chapter 14), and they should also respect the adopter's knowledge of their child.

Birth families cannot be wiped from memory or record

and there is correctly an emphasis on children not being hidden from their birth families. Now that adopted children have the right to seek out records on their birth parents and access to social media to track down those relatives, then supporting children with open and age-appropriate information and connections is even more important than ever.

Note too, that if you adopt a child/ren from a foster family there may be strong bonds there also. You will need to support a child who is grieving for their loss once again after leaving their foster family.

WHAT HAPPENS IF THE BIRTH PARENT WANTS TO REVOKE THE PLACEMENT ORDER?

I think this must be one of the most distressing scenarios of the adoption process. Local authorities have been put in a very difficult position between successive governments demanding more adoptions and courts saying, 'slow down and be more careful'.

If, for whatever reason, the birth parent has decided to challenge the adoption, you can feel that all your hopes and dreams are going to be sabotaged. The amended Children Act 2002 Section 24(2) and (5) covers the requirements of all parties (and you can also look at the Department for Education 2013, para 5.2–5.10).

A birth parent who opposes adoption has two options – both of which will result in the adoption process being delayed. The parent could notify the court that they want to appeal against the placement order. The adoption process will then be in the hands of the birth parent's legal representative and the LA's solicitor. There will be pressure to 'speed' up the process and avoid delays for the benefit of all concerned, especially the child, though realistically this will depend on the agility of your LA's representatives. The birth parent will be required to demonstrate to the court that the decision was wrong or unjust because of serious procedural irregularities.

Secondly, the birth parent can also seek permission to revoke a placement order. For this to succeed, the parent will need to show the court that there has been a 'change of circumstances' with regards to the situation behind the original care order or removal of the child.

Balance has to be found between the LA's adoption plan and the birth parent's rights and the birth parent will have to follow the correct process. For the potential adoptive parent(s), this will be an anxious time. In this situation, another planning meeting will be held to decide what to do about introductions. Should they be postponed, or if the child has already met the adoptive parents, should the relationship continue? How is this to be managed? Also, what if the foster carers are not able to continue to look after the child? One potential step forwards can be when the child could be moved to live with the adopter by approving them as a temporary foster carer under Regulation 25A of the Care Planning Regulations 2010.

This shouldn't happen to you and your child, and you will be aware of the situation around your child's removal from the birth family, so I would hope that you will not have to worry about these circumstances. If it does happen then you, your adoption team and the legal professionals will be working fast and hard to bring these events to a positive outcome.

CHAPTER 13:

Parenting Your Child

Being a parent of an adopted child will require you to think, rethink and think again about what parenting is. Some children grow up with a basic level of security, empathy, resilience and self-regulation but many adopted children have experienced trauma or abuse, directly or indirectly. You will be the child's secure 'safe base' and you will need to become an expert at shrugging off platitudes and interference from everyone. Some of your most beloved family members and friends will see your kindness and patience as weakness: you will hear phrases like 'you need to let her/him know that you're the boss'.

Don't listen. Our children think differently and they may have had to employ survival skills that most marines would be envious of to get through their childhood so far. Parenting an adopted child will be different and you need to embrace that.

> *Do you yell at a flower to grow faster or trust it will in due time?*
> *Let people bloom at their own pace.*
>
> *@wellnessbykarli*

After growing up with trauma myself, and looking after children who have been abused and neglected, I would love to challenge the Department for Education (DfE) to create a measurement that recognises traumatised children's aptitude and emotional agility and other survival skills. I think that would be deeply useful for all of us and enable our children to have the recognition they deserve for the work and energy they have asserted so far to be who they are.

Being separated from your birth family is trauma in itself, never mind what happened prior to that, or subsequent movements in the care system. Adoptive parents need to understand and be skilled to assist the child to self-regulate and get over the horrible sense of shame that comes with abuse and neglect. Your local authority or adoption agency should support you and your family to understand the impact of early life trauma for children and help you consider different ways to respond to adopted children's needs and behaviours.

My biggest recommendation is that I try as much as I can to stick to routines. Mealtimes are roughly the same time each day and I have to spend time helping my child understand and prepare for any change to that. People who have not experienced looking after children with trauma find my behaviour inflexible and obsessive but I am confident and experienced now to know what differences are required for parenting an adopted child.

YOUR OWN CHILDHOOD

You need to be able to reflect in a coherent manner on your own childhood experiences. If you have experienced childhood trauma, or situations in your adult life that are left unspoken with no effort made to resolve them, they will have a substantial negative impact and influence how you treat your child. How did you, and do you, deal with illness, rejection, separation, abuse and loss?

I know an adopted boy, D, now aged 14 years old, who told me that when he was younger his adoptive dad would shout at him. D said he hated this because he remembered his birth dad shouting at his birth mum and his siblings so he didn't like shouting. His adopted mum didn't shout, so one day he told her how his dad's shouting made him feel and how he ended up shouting back and that it just got stupid, that neither of them would back down. His adopted mum said something because his adopted dad stopped and they get on really well together now.

I know that D's adopted dad was devastated when his wife mentioned the shouting. At first he didn't back down as he was stuck in this behaviour. It was only when his wife and adopted son refused to be part of his shouting behaviour by walking away that he sought therapy. As I can't say often enough, we all have stuff, but unresolved childhood issues, if left, can end up being transferred onto our children. When I spoke to the dad, he openly acknowledged that his behaviour was learned from his own father who was blustery and dominant and he thought that was how men should behave. The adopted dad apologised to his wife and, and with the help of his therapist, has now learned strategies to prevent his old behaviour.

Make sure that you and your partner, family and friends have an understanding of what has happened to you. We usually tell the person we have most invested in of our childhood or bad experiences. If you haven't, I strongly advise you do that soon before you start the process. Imagine you are a child stuck in a state of trauma and your new parent, your role model, is avoiding their own issues. If you have not resolved your own issues you will create a toxic environment and your child can believe it's their fault.

I experienced childhood trauma and openly discussed it. The professionals felt I may be a risk and I had the light shone in my face with extra interviews and questions by those assuming that if we suffer trauma we become weak victims or roll over and die. I knew that it wasn't so, and encourage you not to allow any past trauma to derail the adoption process.

If you have experienced trauma you have a gift that needs to be cherished. You will need to advocate for your child and that starts by learning to advocate for yourself – but you must have done the work and demonstrate with absolute authenticity that you are ready. I passionately believe that our frailties and fractures are what make us human and make us suitable for looking after other people's offspring.

REJECTION

I have heard adopters complain that their adopted child resists holding their hand or I hear 'my adopted child won't sit on my lap and read a book'. I have to STOP you right there. Do you need the child to validate to the world that that they love and trust you? How could you know what has happened to your child in the past, perhaps while sitting on an adult's lap? Your child's attachment to you is not a guarantee and most certainly it is a gift. I may sound a little passionate here but a big part of your relationship with your child is to *get over yourselves*. If you are holding onto feelings of rejection because your child isn't performing as you wish then listen carefully: it's not about you. Your child is learning to live with the most primal pain, and rejection is the biggest of them all. They are trying to learn how to live and be with you.

Adopted children have already developed their internal working model. If the child has experienced adverse challenges from their birth family, multiple foster placements and being in the care system they may take longer to respond to your attempts to reach them and develop the beginning of a lifelong attachment, which is why the sooner the child is placed with you – sensitive, resilient-minded, loving parents – then the sooner your child can embrace the opportunity for change in their relationship style. The positive model of relationships that you provide will influence your child's choices and behaviours in all their relationships – with friends, loved ones, employers and so on. When I left my adoption breakdown, I initially chose friends and partners who replaced the negativity and abuse I was used to. I repeated the pain. You can enable your child not to do this.

Rejection is two-way traffic. If you feel it from the child I beg you to resist it and to love them back even more. As the parents we need to help them change the behaviour, not mirror it. If you're worried about rejection from your future child, know that they will be feeling the same about you because they have already experienced rejection and all that brings. Whatever you're feeling, they will likely be feeling it far more deeply than you.

Our children can only articulate their pain through their behaviour. The more you feel they are rejecting you the more this is a plea for you not to. If your child says 'I hate you' they don't hate you, they love you and it's because they feel safe and loved that they can say it now, and they say it for all the times in their life they have felt scared and hurt. It's not always going to be easy but if you recognise that adoption is a topsy-turvy universe, and comparison with other families is futile, you will be in a much better position to adapt your parenting to meet your child's changing needs.

CHILDREN OF DIFFERENT AGES

Challenges will reflect the different ages and stages of your child, but all ages will respond well if you gently keep to a routine as you get to know your child and begin to develop your instincts around them. Realise that your child's emotional age may be much younger than their chronological age so look to provide nurture that is in line with their emotional needs.

Remember your child is new to you, and you to them, so be patient and notice your child's behaviours without flagging up any worries to them. It's generally wise for a new adoptive parent to note that if two or more milestones have not been met by the child then a visit to the GP to discuss your concerns is sensible. I've already noted that every child and family is different, but children from trauma more frequently reach their milestones in an ad hoc way, and sometimes when you least expect it. By providing a safe loving home your child may surprise you and catch up or exceed your expectations.

Babies (newborn to three years old)

If you have a young baby or toddler coming to join your family, I'm sure you will have learned all that you can from friends and family and maybe a few good books (I have recommendations at the end of the book).

Be prepared for the shock of the new to last a few days or weeks – you will feel tired and your child may cry more than usual. Of course, your child will cry and for so many reasons, all babies do. They are in a new environment, missing their foster carers, perhaps can't stand your perfume . . .

Be wise and kind to yourself, limit visitors and work commitments as you will never get this all-too-important time back again. Take it slow and enjoy it, and take plenty of photographs of you and your child – that's very important.

You may want to look into breastfeeding your adopted baby too – it is possible to produce milk even if you have never done so before. As always our strange legal systems complicate matters. For example, if you are fostering to adopt you will not be allowed to breastfeed your baby until you have legally adopted her or him. (Foster carers are not allowed to breastfeed or sleep in bed with children even if that child is in a long-term foster placement with them.) By the time the adoption process is complete your baby may already be weaned. Remember though that there are different ways to feed a child, and 'fed is best'. Please don't compare your family to others – you need to do this your way.

More easy to facilitate, and something that can be enjoyed by adoptive fathers as well as mothers, is skin-to-skin contact – holding your naked baby on your bare chest. This is particularly beneficial for adoptive babies and within minutes you will see the benefits of skin-to-skin as you and your baby relax. Your baby's body temperature, breathing and heart rate will stabilise. Babies often latch on and feed better from a bottle with skin-to-skin contact also. It is a wonderful way to nurture your baby and to bond.

My memory of smell from childhood is still evocative today and I still shiver at the smell of carbolic soap. Smell creates both good and bad memories. I have already flagged that mirroring the foster family's washing detergents to allow for a familiar scent in the child's new home can be

helpful, but look for other ways to bring homely and familiar scents into their new home. Even from a young age, look
for scents that they respond to positively. Your baby needs
to feel familiar with your pheromones and they need to
associate you with happy smells.

Primary school-age children (four to eleven years old)

Whatever the child's age, if they have moved a number of
times before coming to you there will be bad memories,
anxiety and confusion in the front of their minds.

Each of my children in the primary years has pushed
boundaries and I have had to work creatively to find a way
through the issues they present. Bedtime has always been a
touchstone. Many people could not imagine how tense and
impotent we can feel being the parent to a child with attachment issues. I have nicely asked a child to go to bed, and for
half an hour before the agreed bedtime I will have given the
child five-minute updates to ensure that they have no surprises. It doesn't work. I have had full-on rages, violence and
even absconding just because it's bedtime. The rest of the
parenting world would see me as weak, a walkover or possibly
a failure. Trust me when I say 'pick your battles'. If you can
agree on a compromise then go for it. You don't need to feel
that you are winning, you need to feel that you're attaching.

Similarly, I have a laundry basket in my kitchen where I
place folded clean items ready for putting away. One of my
children would go through it looking for his favourite clothes
and always pull everything out and chuck it on the floor. I
am a busy working mother of four children and I would get
so cross! After several months of asking him to be more
careful and considerate and being ignored, I realised that I
was becoming obsessed with this situation and grumpy. It

occurred to me that if I placed his items at the top he could easily access them and I would feel less aggrieved. I am still not sure why it took me so long to resolve this matter but my solution returned the love and harmony once more into my kitchen and life. Pick your battles.

Your young children will struggle with emotional regulation and get stuck in meltdowns or emotional states frequently, and it's important that you create a safe space for them to express themselves. If this is happening to you outside your home please remember that your child's distress is more important than what anyone else thinks. They do not matter.

Your child is expressing their pain and their hurt, their sadness and confusion. They are not doing this to deliberately embarrass you. Stay close by and watch your own body language. Look neutral, put your arms down by your side and work on a calm, kind face. That should help. Your child will hate this more than you, they are out of control and that is scary. They will revisit some of their previous bad times while this is happening. Don't make them feel in the wrong, let them know you care and wait for them to finish. If they create a mess in the process of their meltdown later on you can both clear it away. Your child is more important than broken 'things'.

Teenagers (eleven years old and up)

Most adults forget they were teenagers. I'm puzzled how adults can wipe clean one of the most interesting and scary times of their life. Is it because they were treated without much understanding that they just pass it on?

When I spoke to teenagers, adopted or not, they said they needed to know that their parents were young once too. They struggled to build a trusting relationship with someone who is perfect. Tell them about your past and let them know you can relate to the problems. They would probably like to know that you got into trouble at school or went down the rec with your friends, smoked a cigarette and drank cheap cider. It is a connection, a way into their heart and mind.

I know a couple of teenagers whose adoptions broke down. I was more annoyed than sad that the parents and children didn't get the support or advice that was most needed. One couple had adopted two brothers when they were four and nine years old. The younger child was sporty as well as being a good guitarist but as this young man reached teenage years, his older brother – his rock – left. The younger brother came out as gay, was seriously into music and enjoyed a wild and exciting lifestyle. His adoptive parents complained about his attitude and behaviour, that he was mixing with all the wrong people. In fact the young boy loved music and life, and desperately missed his brother. It's not helpful to a child if their parents have not got a clue about their lives. Let's be honest, 'they're a different generation' and they do their lives differently, so a compromise is the best any of us can ask for.

Try not to let 'boring' be the root to problems. That's when your adopted child may feel that you don't understand them and being misunderstood is a lonely place for a teenager. Factor in adoption and unresolved issues on both sides and you have a lovely mess on its way. I'm not saying that you need to understand Drill music but do show some interest in who your child is becoming. I live with a number of teenagers who all have different musical tastes, I can walk through my house and feel like I'm in a nightclub. I love it! I enjoy their company and the company of their friends. They hang out near the fridge and eat me out of house and home and their rooms are never tidy but they choose to be here and I know they are safe.

Sometimes I think the notion of parenting has changed. We are still bed makers and bottle washers but because our children are connected to a virtual world we spend a lot of time serving as the home police of the internet. External influences are bigger and more out of our reach than ever. Before they are let loose in your home with social media, even if they have been using it in their foster placement or wherever, they need to be clear about the following:

- Make sure that they don't publish personal information such as their location, email address, phone number or date of birth
- Ensure your child is very careful about what images and messages they post, even among trusted friends – once they are online they can be shared widely and are extremely difficult to remove
- Encourage them to talk to you if they come across anything they find offensive or upsetting.

I think we are now moving past the stage when we thought that our children having access to the internet felt like the end of the world. I can't tell you how worried I was about social media and then I did something incredible; I began to trust my children. I realised that what I can do is educate my children, along with good support from their schools, and we can do the best we can to keep our children safe.

Yes, our adopted children have tendencies to take greater risks – I can vouch for that personally – but they're also capable of making good decisions when the choices are laid out clearly in front of them without threat or punity.

Finally, remember also that the strongest attachments are often made when we are recovering from an argument, meltdown or incident. You are an adoptive parent with a child who needs constant validation that you love them and have their back – and you can do that.

Sibling groups

I have looked after sibling groups and they bring different challenges to a placement – individually and together. If the parents had not been present, or could not meet the children's needs, the eldest child often stepped in and assumed many of the parenting roles. This can be hard on them because they may have missed out on their own childhood, and they may still think and behave like the parent when they are in placement and undermine the parenting role and style of their new adopted parents, therefore creating tensions.

I have known children ask to be placed separately because they recognise that they need a break and time to be themselves. Some people feel that separating a sibling group is an outrageous idea but it's never done lightly and only if enough professionals feel that it is the right decision. Part of the decision process would include positive contact with the siblings.

YOUR NEEDS VS THE CHILD'S NEEDS

Adoptive parenting demands that we need to be even more aware of ourselves in all our attachments, to be aware of what we need and want from our relationship with our child.

When I first began my journey of looking after other people's offspring, I remember sitting in a training session listening to yet another 'guru' explain that 'it can take up to ten years to help a child recover from trauma. You have to create a lifestyle that is consistent, calm and quiet, you can no longer be spontaneous'.

'What? I am not that person!'

Luckily, when I heard that, I had been looking after other people's children long enough to know that it doesn't have to be like that. I would like adoptive parents to relax. Much of the advice for parents is written for the 'ideal world'.

You will hear phrases like 'conscious parenting', which can be very confusing. I started my training with this theory and I mulled it over in my head for years. It centres around looking at ourselves – the idea of our own egos, beliefs and attachments and how they influence the relationship – as the cause of many parenting issues, rather than the child. Sometimes the gap between completing and needing the training can be ages. And if you're like me you may well have forgotten a lot of what you learned by the time you need it and do a sort of 'version of' which may not always be helpful. It's a resounding flaw in adoption and fostering training, an assumption that attending the sessions means that you know what you're doing. I now take the bits that work for me and my children and have stopped beating myself up because I can't remember everything.

It began to dawn on me that after the various versions of attachment training I was part of a cohort of parents who were 'self-consciously parenting'. The levels of prescriptive advice were sometimes overwhelming. I compare it to

telling a natural free-flowing dancer how to dance by following a new sequence of moves from an instruction
manual. The moves become stilted and self-conscious, not
helped by also feeling observed and judged. What 'conscious parenting' had done to mere mortals like myself who
do the day-in-day-out care of our children was make us feel
inadequate. If we didn't manage to line up all the ducks in
the right order we had failed. I think we struggle with having our intuitive parenting responses scrutinised.

I take the view that, on the whole, most people who
come forward to adopt already recognise their parenting
instincts. You will know if expressions like 'go and sit on the
thinking bean bag' will not work for you. They don't for
me. That's not how I speak or who I am. The same with
calling the child's birth mother 'tummy mummy'; I'm
happy with the fact that it's just NOT my thing.

So we need to find our own voice to be able to work with
authenticity and meaning. I draw on attachment theories
for inspiration and ideas but our children need confident
parents and they need, most of all, to feel safe. We should
not be living in fear of being caught out and punished
because we swear or raise our voice. We are human beings
who live and work with children who many of our judgemental acquaintances could not.

I'm not an expert in attachment and I wanted to get my
information right so I asked a few people I would rate as
being as close to an expert on the subject of attachment as
possible. If you want to know about attachment, ask children. I asked children and young people who are adopted.

P was in foster care for two years. He had moved placements three times. When he went to live with his adoptive family, he was seven years old.

Me. Do you remember how you felt before and when you met your adopted parents?

P. I thought it would be like another foster home. I thought there was going to be loads of rules and a small bedroom.

Me. What did you know about your adopted parents before you met the parents and children?

P. I knew they had other children, I thought they were going to be horrible to me.

Me. How did you feel when you met your parents and children?

P. I was scared, I thought the children would be mean and tease me. I thought my new parents would let them get away with it. I remember A, who is also adopted, giving me some sweets; she was nice. The others were as scared as me. My new mum had and has the biggest warmest smile I had ever seen, my new dad looked kind.

Me. What makes someone look kind?

P. He wasn't in my face, he didn't look angry. He looked soft and looked like he would know how to mend my bike.

Part of the 'My Story' research is having these conversations. When your child has been with you long enough and you feel they are ready it would be good to reflect on how they remember the build-up before they came to live with you and how they felt when they met you.

S is 12 years old and has been in her adopted family for two years. She was the oldest of her sibling group. Originally her care plan was for her to remain in foster care while her younger siblings were adopted. Due to early life trauma and the chaotic and sometimes toxic dynamic between her and her three siblings, it was decided that the group should split up and be placed separately.

Me. When you knew that you were going to be adopted what did you think?

S. I was worried and felt upset. Everyone kept going on about how scared I must be feeling. I wasn't scared. I was actually excited but felt guilty. I was sad to leave my foster carers — they had been nice and helped me. I got fed up with being told how I must be feeling, I didn't know. I think I was more overwhelmed by all the information and conversations from the adults. I just wanted it to happen and be left alone.

Me. How did you feel when you were told by your social worker that you were going to be adopted?

S. I was happy and angry. I knew my brothers and sisters were going to be adopted and I guess I felt jealous. No one wanted me, I was too old, too ugly, too stupid. I wanted a mum, I really did. I use to watch my friends at school with their mums, they would go shopping and all that, I wanted that as well.

Me. What did you think when you met your adopted mum?

S. I was really worried that she would be religious, and strict. I do swear and all that, I didn't want to be told off because I would have lost it and run away. I thought she would be bossy but she wasn't. She was nice. She was not strict and she didn't tell me off even when I broke stuff. She sat next to me and waited for me to calm down. I liked it, I felt safe.

The children I met were decisive and clear about their views and feelings, about being in the care system and their adoptions. I picked up that their main fear was that adopted parents were going to be strict or impose their views or habits. After unpicking this, I think many children have a view about politics, race, money and religion passed onto them by their families

When I asked the children about how they felt about their attachment to their adoptive parent(s) I received some of the best advice for adopters I could ever have wished for.

The children knew they would have days when their behaviour would be expressing their deepest emotions and memories. If the children are not babies when they come to live with you they will have been near behaviour and attitudes that may make the hairs on your neck stand up. It is their past and it is not their fault. I have never met a child who went to bed and woke up plotting a way to upset you. Those children belong in films and books. Most children I have met, lived with and worked with, want the opportunity to be good. When they are good, they feel good. One nine-year-old told me that her adopted parents sat her down after she arrived (then aged six) and told her, 'We are new to this too, and if we make mistakes we will do our best to make them right so that we can work together'. The little girl loved this approach and she felt part of an adventure, a partnership.

My children like it when I share age-appropriate scenarios from my childhood, as all children do. I tell them about my mistakes, my emotions and my adventures. It's okay to be human, parenting is by osmosis.

I remember attending a parenting training session (usually 'death by PowerPoint') where we were advised to put in 'consequences' for children whose behaviour had been challenging. Not long after, one of my children, who had experienced trauma in his early life, had a complete meltdown. After pushing over two kitchen chairs he stomped off to his room and pulled it apart. I stood downstairs wondering if he had broken his PlayStation and TV that we bought him for Christmas. Eventually the crashing, banging and grunting died down so I went upstairs and knocked on his door. I slowly entered his room. He was standing by the window breathing heavily. He looked at me and I looked at him. I walked over to him, and gave him a big hug. We both burst into tears. Trauma isn't straightforward – it's fragile and painful.

I asked him if he was hungry. He said 'no' but followed me down to the kitchen where I made him some waffles and a drink. Our children need to let off steam and scream out their pain. Sometimes we will never know what 'triggers' our children and that's fine. We are not magicians but should follow our caring instincts. If I had dealt with him as that training session had suggested I could have lost him.

After that day I scrapped behaviour and reward charts and consequences. Now I play it by ear. When my children are good or just being themselves and happy I treat them. When they're struggling I support them. Sometimes they are so scared of us and themselves they become defensive. I try to understand how they feel. I remember how I felt when I was a child. This is when you need to be brave. Trust your instinct. You are their parent.

> *If you think you will be a good adopter because you have worked with children or young people please forget everything you think you know and start again, with the child in front of you.*
>
> *Adoptee (teenager)*

When we look after other people's offspring we do bear a certain amount of scrutiny that other parents would not have to tolerate. I have seen some adopters micro-manage their child and I wonder if the need to do this is more about the adults' need to have control or perhaps a way of managing their own anxiety. I have listened to myself sometimes and wondered why I was saying 'no'. Was it the right parent response, because I was tired or because I was worried about being judged? Often it is a mix of all these things.

You likely already have valuable parenting skills and

experience but adopting a child will test your emotions and your resolve. Our children are individuals with different interests, characters and needs and we respond accordingly.

Here are my four top tips to get you through the first six months:

- Spend your time and resources on what's important.
- Don't worry that you are 'spoiling' your child because you are responding to their cries and behaviours. You are developing trust.
- Routines are important to all of us, we need to know what we're doing. So do our children.
- Find things to talk about. One of the greatest regrets parents of adopted children have, particularly after a disturbance, is the realisation that they had stopped talking with their child, they became strangers. Keep lines of communication open.

SELF CARE

Finally, I want to emphasise how important it is to spend time on yourself and look after yourself throughout the adoption process, especially once your child has moved in and the next stage is underway.

I think of this scenario: when you are flying, the flight attendant demonstrates that the adult needs to put their own mask on first before helping any others, including their children. Simply because if you don't you will die and so will the others around you. You need to look after yourself. You need to feel physically well, because you can never be prepared enough for the dramatic new use of your energy, both physically and mentally.

All parents can run themselves ragged trying to be the best parents they can and I have learned that some things are not worth worrying about or can be done later. What is important is the here and now. If you want to shout and scream at an inanimate object then go for it, as long as it's not a person or a pet. Those people who choose to adopt often have character traits that naturally lead them to care first about the needs of others. This means they may tie themselves in knots by putting others' issues before their own needs. I plead with you to take care of yourself as well.

My list for survival is quite obvious, but adopters tend to forget this in the excitement and anxiety of a new child's arrival:

- Get enough rest
- Exercise regularly
- Eat well – good food, fruit and vegetables
- Have your health checks with your GP.

With regards to your ongoing mental health, find some regular mindful activity that you can fit into your schedule – activities that do not ask a lot of you and that allow you to zone out. Keep talking to those who support you and make you feel lighter.

I also enjoy staring at the washing machine cycle going around and watching the washing blowing on the line. I'm a cheap date!

CHAPTER 14:

Life Story/My Story Work

Finally in this section, I want to talk about something simple but very significant in your new child's life . . . Your child will arrive with a little book (or file), as all LAs have a statutory duty to provide every child who is to be adopted with a 'Life Story' book. This will be a record of the child's life so far – including significant information about the birth family and any subsequent foster carers in an age-appropriate way. When children in care can move around geographically and move through several foster placements and social workers, it is helpful for the child to have written and photographic records that support their memories and put their history in context – from photographs and details of people and places to tickets and letters. The book will have been started by an early social worker, and other members of their team, including previous foster carers, may have contributed.

I always suggest that when you receive this, you have a private look to see if it's useful. If it contains information that you don't think your child is ready to see yet or needs then keep it under a pile of bedding in the airing cupboard, or a place where your child will not find it. (I still feel frustrated that my adoption file had mine and my adoptive parents' names consistently spelled differently.) If it's positive and contains good photos of your child's birth family with helpful information, then you have something to build on.

One of the main reasons for the variation in quality is that this work is left to individual social workers to complete and they have too much work already (the task is often handed over to the assistant or undergraduate on work experience). I think it would be great if each LA employed a dedicated member of staff who was trained and enthusiastic to work on these books. And when we say books I have seen a few laminated pieces of A4 paper calling itself a 'Life Story' – imagine what it must feel like to receive such a flimsy account of your previous life.

More recently the book become the responsibility of the adopted parent. I'm pleased about this as you will know your child better than anyone else and can ensure that the information is accurate (using the word 'accurate' in broad terms) and represents a realistic and accessible support for your child.

Every day of our child's life is an active Life Story scenario; it's what's happening now as much as what happened in their past. A good Life Story can:

- Help your child build a sense of identity
- Enhance self-esteem and self-worth
- Give details and understanding of a child's history
- Share a child's past/future with others
- Give a realistic account of early experiences and help to dispel any fantasies about birth families
- Help resolve issues of separation and loss.

The Life Story book is given to the child and prospective adopters in stages, and the completed book within ten working days of the adoption ceremony, or earlier.

THE TRUTH IS IMPORTANT

The truth is the Holy Grail in adoption; we need to know all we can about our child's past, for our sakes and definitely for theirs. I heard many versions of the apparent truth of my birth history growing up and as I got to know my birth mother (I never met my birth father) I heard another set of narratives. My head was in a spin. WHO AM I? This became my underlying identity crisis for the first half of my life.

It took me until I had my first birth child to stop questioning my heritage and physical identity. I could have been saved so much pain and poor self-esteem if someone had recognised that knowing the truth about my identity was important.

Some adopters have asked me if they should tell the truth about their child's past life. We adopt children who cannot live with their birth families for whatever reason. I strongly believe that the truth, without prejudice, without an agenda, is the right way to talk to our children.

If your adopted child was born in difficult circumstances – perhaps out of rape – tell them; if their birth mother had a mental health problem, tell them; if there were drugs, alcohol and crime tell them (further on in this section I explain how to give difficult news to an adopted children). With social media, semi-open and open adoptions, our children will find out information and may directly approach their birth family. The information should come from you with your love and support.

WORKING ON THE MY STORY BOOK

This is one of the most important activities you and your child can do together. No other children have to learn about themselves this way and, in my opinion, its reinforces their sense of difference. I prefer 'My Story' to 'Life Story' or 'Life Work' – nothing about this should be laborious. It should feel like fun – only engage in this activity when you're both in the right mood and have the time.

Continue the book given to you, or begin a new book (for example, an A3 hardback sketchbook with good-quality paper, which can be bought from most art suppliers and online). Write 'Book 1' on the front in big letters, then Book 2, on the next book and so on. It's a lifetime's work.

Illustrate and decorate the pages with photographs, illustrations and drawings, and add coloured ribbons or extras to enhance the presentation. You want your child to enjoy and give to the book, to engage with the recording of their present. (Please never refer to My Story as a scrapbook: the words 'scrap', 'damaged' and 'broken' need to be kept away from our children. They help no one.) Ensure that key names, dates and details are incorporated – My Story is written in the third person, as if narrated by another referring to your child and others by name and he/she/they.

The intention of making the book is to have a lifelong reference for your child to take with them through life. If they help you make it, that shared memory will help deepen their understanding of their past and their present. We get ours out to work on whenever my child has the inspiration or we have learned something new.

As you work through your child's My Story book, make sure to add plenty of subliminal messages about your child being loved, and how they are valued for who they are. Use phrases such as 'aren't you interesting?', 'you have a fascinating history' or 'wow, your grandparents came from Peru – isn't that wonderful?' as you create it together.

The best My Story books I have seen do not shut easily; they are fat and bulky with bits sticking out here and there. They smell of glue and nice paper or perhaps a chocolate wrapper or favourite perfume, aromatic garden leaves and so on. (We have already talked about the positive power of scent to give our children a sense of calm which can later trigger happy memories.)

You are the parent; you are their most important person and they are yours. You could start with what you did today.

WHAT SHOULD THE MY STORY BOOK CONTAIN?

Information for the book can be collected from all those who are in your child's team – from their birth family/relatives to their social worker and foster carer, their Independent Reviewing Officer (IRO) and, most importantly, from YOU.

Photographs will be key to your child's memory. When I found my adopted brother ten years ago he told me that he hadn't got one photograph of himself as a baby or child. Photographs are such powerful conveyors of information and memory keepers – keep originals safe and scan them for use in the book. You can get your child to take photographs too.

You could create a **ME Spread** – stick a big, bright happy picture of your child in the middle of two pages. Draw lines from their picture to other key people. You and their adoptive family are first – you are their family. Using more lines and arrows add pictures of their birth family, social workers and friends – everyone who is important in your child's life in this moment. Record names and little comments (it's good practice to only use first names to protect your child from searching for people before they are ready). As the books grow in number, add updated images of relevant people.

A scan of a **Later Life Letter**, written by your child's social worker, foster carer or other key people in your child's past life about how/why they were taken into care and adopted is important. Never underestimate the relevance of someone noticing and caring about them enough to write a letter about their memories of them. It's all ratification that your child matters.

Your child's **Child Permanence Report** could also be scanned and added.

I asked and asked for my child's information, it took a lot of nagging and emails but we got what we needed to fill the gaps. It's the social worker's job to supply you with information, sometimes I had to stamp my feet!
Rhiannon, adoptive mum

OTHER CREATIVE PROJECTS

This may prompt you to find other ways to help your child to view their journey:

Keep photographs on display – so that your child gets used to seeing faces of family members, and encourage any conversations that these photographs prompt.

The long and winding road – some adopters I know

have used a roll of wallpaper lining paper to explain their lives. It is truly magical!

Memory Boxes – can hold a collection of artefacts we had collected so far: milk teeth, locks of hair, a ticket from the cinema, the wrapping from their first aeroplane meal, important birthday cards, pebbles and shells from the beach or certificates from school, you know the sort of thing.

The My Story book is never finished. Children need to return to and revaluate difficult events as they progress developmentally and at important transitions such as changing schools or if you move house.

As you learn more about and understand your child's past you will feel an enormous amount of empathy that will generate a deeper love and trust between you, and a better sense of security and permanence for your child. Creating a My Story book stresses the child's need to feel claimed and to belong. It raises the adoptive parents' profile and emphasises the child's importance. What's not to like?

PART FOUR

What Could Possibly Go Wrong?

CHAPTER 15:

Bumps in the Road Ahead

Looking after a child who has experienced early life trauma is a bit like playing Whack-a-Mole. Just as you think you have dealt with one issue, another pops up. Stamina and positivity are going to be essential for the road ahead.

In theory, of course, nothing should go wrong. You have been educated and trained and understand the needs of children who have experienced adversity. You have fantastic support from your LA or adoption agency. Your child is the apple of your eye(s) and displays no challenging behaviour. Yet, according to Adoption UK, up to 65 per cent of adoptive families experience violence or aggression. It is nearly impossible to find statistics about the number of adoption breakdowns, which makes me suspicious . . .

From my experience, and speaking to seasoned adopters, I see a pattern of events and challenges that I want you to be aware of. I will discuss some options and choices that can help change situations and avoid the deterioration of relationships.

Starting at the very beginning – did the information you

were given by the adoption team tell you everything you needed to know about your child? Do you feel that you have a full grasp on your child's pre-birth experiences, their birth family, their educational needs and their emotional developmental needs now, and for the future?

> *We adopted Reggie when he was three years old. He was a happy and content little boy. We could never have imagined what an explosion of challenging and risk-taking behaviours would be unleashed when he hit puberty. He became a different child and, worse still, he became violent.*
>
> *Lynda, adoptive mum*

What happened to Reggie and Lynda has happened to many adoptive parents and their children. Reggie's birth mother had taken drugs and alcohol while she was pregnant with Reggie and the effects of foetal damage don't always present while the child is young; they can burst into action when a child begins their teenage years. Reggie displayed 'avoidance attachment' from around twelve years old. Lynda had not been told about Reggie's birth mum's substance abuse so was not prepared for its effects on him. As she was not aware of his pre-birth experiences (it had somehow not been included in his files), she did not take the necessary steps to apply for support and funding before they were in crisis. Lynda and Reggie managed to work and live through his challenges but with great emotional and financial cost. When you are in a crisis with your child and submitting an application for funding to enable therapeutic support (factoring in that the application will probably take months, if not years, to be approved) then you will be forced to draw on your personal resources. Sadly, when an adoption faces 'disruption' or breakdown – adoptions are described as 'intact' or 'disruptive' – the LA may not be supportive and your parenting skills may be criticised. This is not fair or helpful but we cannot change the children's social care culture. If you can plan ahead, hopefully you will avoid a level of disruption in your family.

Finding and funding therapy for your child is covered in Part Three, but it is also important that you, the adopter(s), are looked after. Whether it's mild provocative behaviour from a struggling toddler or more violent reactions from a child as big as you, I have seen strong, good people reduced to emotional wrecks while they wade through the treacle of trying to make sense of their child's extreme behaviour. I'm not going to patronise you with techniques for yoga and purchases of scented candles. I have been there and I have sat alone in the garden on a cold evening wondering how my life ended up like this, knowing that I could not escape the child who made me feel under siege. An eight-year-old girl has held me at knifepoint; I've been hit and kicked by a ten-year-old boy until I was black and blue, and I was slapped so hard round the face by a thirteen-year-old girl that I thought my nose was going to fall off. The police noted these events as 'domestic abuse' and, though we want to support our children, we also need to protect and look after ourselves.

If things become tricky in your family, don't feel that you have failed. You haven't. I would love to see the professionals who offer easy platitudes or direct/indirect criticism do what we do. If you have a good social worker, who doesn't sit there writing down everything you say, but offers to take your child out to give you a break or who works hard to get you and your child proper support, then treasure them and work with them. It can be hard to know whom to trust when you have hit crisis point.

I have lost contact with friends who didn't understand and I have lived in fear of being judged or receiving allegations from the professionals who are meant to support us, but I found great support from teachers and fellow adopters/carers. There are websites, Facebook groups and blogs providing information about places where you will be able to discuss your situation with those who understand. While your life is calm, it is vital you create your own networks and friendships with people who 'get it'. You are not alone.

Sometimes our lives get in the way too. Living with a challenging child can raise issues in our own relationships. It's a big ask to work on your relationship while your own identity is being challenged but keep trying to find the time and space for balance in your life. All storms pass . . .

When we parents need to feel calm and safe to support our spiralling children, we can also lose perspective and control – and there is only one direction that toxic soup will go.

'COMPASSION FATIGUE' AND 'BLOCKED CARE'

In children's social care the terms 'blocked care' and 'compassion fatigue' are common terms that you will come across on your parenting courses, representing parent's potential behaviour and emotions towards their child. They are often used when a placement begins to break down.

'Compassion fatigue' is when parenting a child with trauma causes significant stress in the parent, and this is used alongside 'blocked care' to put a name to a state when parents are unable to connect with their child, when prolonged stress suppresses the capacity to sustain loving and empathic feelings towards the child. Both terms are used by social care professionals to describe the same thing. Unfortunately, terms are often invented by academics that sound clinical and inhumane and which don't help the parent to understand what is happening or allow for the fact that it is a vulnerable child who is being discussed.

There is much research and guidance around these subjects and the advice is useful and well-intended but it doesn't include the elephant in the room – the lack of support for the adopter and adoptee is key in these experiences. I never want any of you to experience the pain and hurt of an adoption breakdown.

Your child's behaviour may be showing itself as fearful, deregulated and extremely challenging and you may have reached the point where you are consciously or subconsciously protecting and separating yourself from their trauma. It's two-way traffic. You may even be aware of your own behaviour, but when a professional remarks that you are suffering from 'blocked care' or 'compassion fatigue', it can feel like a criticism.

After talking with many adopters who have, or are going through adoption disruptions, I need to be clear that the disruptions tend to occur after the parent(s) have asked for help and had little in response. As a long-term foster carer, the difference between this and adoption is clear to me – when you adopt, the LA tends to walk away and leave you alone. With foster care, the corporate parent (LA/agency) is legally required to respond to health and educational needs. Some are better than others. My concern is that adopters are labelled with 'blocked care' or 'compassion fatigue' when part of the problem is the parents' battle with the system to get their child's needs recognised.

I have experienced this and it was horrible. I was exhausted, and on occasion I couldn't deal with the child. I felt ill, devalued and, when I asked for help, I was met with an attitude from my social workers and their managers that I was not coping, I was failing. I realised later, that when I was in this state, I was completely exhausted and was protecting my family and myself from the child's trauma. The child's behaviour was playing out as out of control and violent and I only had the energy to react to their outbursts. I couldn't keep digging within myself to find more compassion and empathy to support the child's emotional needs. I saw my child sinking into crisis, as was I. This is when we need support.

If you feel your LA or agency isn't recognising your needs, again you must look for other support networks that you can tap into, often with parents who have experienced these situations themselves.

Most adopters I spoke to recognised that they were in 'compassion fatigue' or 'blocked care' and found the platitudes and criticism from professionals more harmful to their situation than the experience and recognition of their circumstances. My plea to the professionals is to please stop the criticism. Roll up your sleeves and get stuck into some good old-fashioned social work and help the family through these dark times. Every disruption or breakdown is a human tragedy for all involved.

Couldn't you have got one with less problems?

Adopter's sister

THE 'HONEYMOON PERIOD'

Experts often call the first weeks and months of an adoption the 'honeymoon period'. Honeymoons themselves are a time to relax, reflect and have some fun. An adoptive child's 'honeymoon' has probably meant saying goodbye to several key people in their lives, having tons of reports written about them and people deciding what's best for them. As a result, I feel that 'honeymoon' is one of those words that children's social care use lazily to describe something that is actually quite serious. What I have seen in the 'honeymoon period' is a series of behaviours and emotions that are really very powerful and full of hope.

Children from trauma will assess new people in a primal way. We want to know if you are safe, we need to learn as much about your character and personality as quickly as possible. I have heard adults talk about their new child following them with their eyes, observing every detail. 'Of course', I say, 'what would you do if you had no power and needed to live as well and safely as you could?'.

These children have seen adults out of control, abusive and cruel, so they need to learn you and learn fast. They may set up little tests to ascertain how you react to things – 'pushing boundaries' – but I beg you to see it from their point of view. They're not trying to find your weaknesses; they're actually trying to find your strengths and to see how you respond to things. I have been in this situation many times before with children and teenagers who have come into my care. When they are describing self-harming or becoming a prostitute when they grow up, I tend to look for gentle distractions away from their provoking comments.

I remember my husband being shouted at by a child explicitly describing gay sex as he sat quietly, and when she had finished trying to shock and get a rise out of him, he said, 'Thanks for telling me that – I didn't know. Would you like a cup of tea?'.

Many children also go on a charm offensive and behave in a perpetually positive and thoughtful manner, constantly on their best behaviour. They naïvely think this will endear them to you. They are not being devious or trying to lull you into a false sense of security, they are genuinely trying to decide if they can love and trust you.

It's SURVIVAL at the end of the day. On some level, your child will know that if this goes wrong, you will be alright but they could end up literally anywhere and with anyone. I have been that child and I learned survival skills that others would perceive as deceptive or manipulative but I was just trying to survive.

When your child truly believes that you love them unconditionally the testing behaviours will drop away.

POO AND WEE

I attended one training session where a psychologist led a session about traumatised children and poo. What I remember most from this session were the reactions from the other attendees who were clearly baffled and revolted by the idea of poo as a way for children to express their emotions. As an ex-'poo user' myself, I felt ashamed by their reaction. After the coffee break that day I decided that I would not be shamed and, on behalf of all the children who will be in their care, I decided to speak up. When we went back into the session I raised my hand and told them, 'I used to poo in strange places, and I enjoyed holding my poo in my hand and squeezing it'. Everyone, including the psychologist, looked horrified and I resisted the old feeling of shame and I sat there with a determined look of 'what's your problem'.

Apart from confirming my belief that most people, including some professionals, cannot see the adopted child as an adult. (They must think that we will be poo users for the rest of our lives.) Because I was terrified of my adopted mum I would take myself off to the back of my adopted dad's garage where there was a surplus of gravel at the end. I would make a hole with my foot, do my business and, just like a cat, I buried it. I also smeared poo under my adopted mum's bed hoping that she would smell it in the night as a subconscious act of protest. I was too young to know what a protest was.

All behaviour is communication – this is crucial to remember when things become difficult. If your child comes to your home and begins to poo and wee in unusual places, please don't panic. They are letting you know that they feel anxious and that saying goodbye to people they may have loved and moving into your home is pretty big stuff. They are just saying 'help'.

You may be disgusted. You may be furious. But why? Put yourself in their shoes and think about how you would feel if you continuously had no control over your own life. Wouldn't the control of your own bowels feel like something significant?

If you adopt a younger child who has been toilet trained, or if you are doing this work, your child may relapse. This is normal, just keep going with the routine and you will get back on track. At some point you could have a chat with your GP if you are still concerned but, like me, your child may find this is the only form of self-expression they have right now, as well as giving them a sense of control that they do need.

You may also experience bedwetting. (If your child has been diagnosed as having ADHD or you are beginning to suspect this, note that it is common for children with this disorder to be bedwetters.) Ask first whether your child wet the bed before they came to live with you. Did they share a room? Are they missing their roommate? Does their new room feel too different? It may be worth asking their foster carer about the layout and maybe the colours to see if you can make their sleeping area feel more secure for them. There are also practical items you can buy to save your mattress and bedding, as well your child wearing pull-ups, if necessary.

Please, please, please, don't ask your child *why* they are doing this.

They won't know why it is happening, it's just what works for them at the moment. You are not going to get a rational answer. You could ask them a direct question and they may skirt round it with what you feel is a 'lie' but they are not liars, they are just scared to tell you their truth because they don't understand it and feel ashamed. Calling them a liar will enforce that shame which will mutate into other shame.

While you feel cross and tired at dealing with their poo and wee, focus on remembering that your child is feeling rage, sorrow, helplessness, hopelessness, profound sadness, frustration and loneliness. Compared to a little extra washing, it's not the same, so listen and watch your child's behaviour because they are speaking to you.

Instead of waking up in the morning thinking, 'I bet I

have to clean up again', wake up and think 'my child is sad and I will do all I can to not shame her/him but to love them more'.

Try activities that help your child feel positive about themselves and their toileting. Slowly and with kindness, teach your child your house hygiene rules, and make it light-hearted. Get them to be the loo roll monitor perhaps, or encourage them to choose a new item to decorate the loo or bathroom.

* * *

Imagine how much physical and mental and emotional energy is involved in a child's first few months in a new home and family. Survival is not a relaxing activity and your child's behaviour may deteriorate because they are exhausted. They may be so scared of letting you down or finding new ways to test that you won't let them down that they struggle to keep it together a lot of the time. Similarly, you need to keep up as well and not burn out. My advice would be to keep your first few weeks and months as simple as you can, gently introducing your expectations and expecting a few wobbles.

CHAPTER 16:

Discipline and Dealing with Violence

Violence is the result of a combination of biological, social and psychological factors, especially those that increase exposure to vulnerability, shame and humiliation. Preventing violence must involve the opposite: making sure people feel safe, cared about and connected, while ensuring they have a healthy and realistic sense of self-esteem and self-worth.

Dr Lisa Firestone

I remember sitting in my kitchen with a police officer after weeks of what felt like a planned campaign from an eight-year-old boy. He terrorised us and we were scared of him. A small person can be as frightening as a big person. We had bruises, cuts and broken furniture, and we were completely exhausted. The policeman strongly disagreed with the social worker's view on trauma. He said 'living with a traumatised child who is violent is the same as living with anyone who lashes out, manipulates and wants to control. It's domestic abuse'. When a child is violent, not enough people take it seriously, particularly if the child is young. It was the policeman who enabled us to understand that we were the victims.

Violence can give a child power where they feel like they have none.

R. Cook, GP

I, too, became violent as a little girl. At the time I had undiagnosed dyslexia and could not express myself well. I had been placed in the remedial group at school and I was terrified of my life at home with my adopted family. I did not feel safe but could not articulate this. I was 'shooting from my inner child's emotional hip', reacting to how I was feeling. I remember a need to smash things, to pull and break objects, to scream and shout and to cry. It felt good. The outcome looked like violence but it was nothing compared to the violence that had been inflicted onto me, both passively and physically, from birth.

If the child is using violence to get what they want and need, then they have learned that they are powerful when they are violent. Obviously this has to stop for so many reasons. We have to influence and teach them to learn better life skills. If you show you're struggling, that you have had enough and that you need external help or are threatening to end your relationship with them, then you must expect more violence. Our first job is to reassure. Remember your initial commitment to your child. If they feel that this is breaking they will want you to break with them.

Preparing our children to be happy, balanced adults is

our job. Part of our daily work is to teach our children that abuse is wrong. Our children are accountable, just like we are. If we speed and get stopped we have to either pay a fine or go on a training course to make us safer drivers. It's the same with our children. If your child is violent, accountability is essential to them understanding the seriousness of their actions. We need to break the pattern, and new better ones need to be learned.

CONSEQUENCES ARE BETTER THAN PUNISHMENT

It's tempting to deliver a harsh punishment when your child has broken a rule. You might feel compelled to send the message: 'I'm your parent. You need to listen to me'. Unfortunately, punishments are not an effective way to change behaviour, nor are they a constructive way to reassert your parental authority.

Know the difference between a punishment and a consequence. A punishment is retribution (or vengeance) for a wrongful act. Consequences are usually natural or logical outcomes that result from one's behaviour. You can't punish your child into good behaviour, but you can get them to want to behave better through effective consequences.

A consequence might be the loss of a privilege until your child completes a task or behaves acceptably for a specified period of time. This isn't a punishment, although it may feel like one to your child. A good consequence is tied to the behaviour in such a way that if the behaviour improves, the consequence goes away as a result – something that follows naturally from a person's action, inaction, or poor decision, intended to teach or modify behaviour in a positive way.

The right consequence should actually motivate your child to good behaviour. It puts you back in control and teaches your child how to problem-solve, giving your child the skills needed to be a successful adult. That's what we want!

I also ask you to reflect on your own behaviour. I am aware that adults can struggle with acknowledging that they may have made mistakes. It's difficult knowing that our child's birth family and the social care system is watching us. Once we start blaming we become further and further away from our child and their needs. Try to hold the thought in your head that the more the child is behaving badly or violently, the more they are trying to tell you just how bad, confused and scared they feel. That's easier said than done if your child is over six feet tall and trashing the house. We'll come onto that later.

I have often explained the consequence to a child who then looks at me and says, 'I don't care'. What they really mean is: 'I am going to attempt to distract you with my maturity and indifference'. So far I have not met a child who genuinely didn't care. The more they say it the more I know they do care that we love them and support them. I have heard 'I don't care' through words, broken objects, door slamming and angry eye rolls. Be brave, stand firm and stick to your consequence.

TASKS ARE BETTER THAN PUNISHMENTS

A 'task-oriented consequence' both relates to the offence and defines a learning objective. For example, if your child stays out past curfew then insist that the next two times they go out they have to come in an hour earlier to show you that they can do it. If this happens, you can revert to the normal curfew time. Similarly, broken furniture or thrown dishes can be 'mended' with time clearing up the garden or being responsible for clearing the table for one week.

In contrast, grounding them for a month will not teach them to observe a curfew or to be more respectful of your things. It just puts you and your family through grief and the child learns nothing and is not incentivised to revise their behaviour. Ask yourself: if you make a mistake at work, would you rather be publicly punished and humiliated or would you like to experience kind advice and the chance to correct and improve your work?

Ensure that your child understands that you have given them a specific length of time by which they need to complete the task. The length of time should be long enough so your child has time to think about what they've done, but not so long that they lose interest and give up or become angry. Then you will be back at the beginning.

Be fair with the impact and size of the consequence for the problem. I have made my children sweep leaves, vacuum floors, weed my garden and so on. I only asked them to start once I had shown them what to do and set expectations. It is important that you ask for a standard of work from the task. Often children rise to the challenge. Some have thrown themselves on the floor sobbing, 'Why are you making me do this?'. If I have not explained the purpose of the consequence clearly enough I try again and again until the message is understood.

Remember all consequences will require your commitment and time, but the shorter the better in my opinion. If you do something for days at a time you will lose interest and also respect from your child.

Don't fear appearing weak or soft if your consequences seem mild compared to the act. Remember that comparison to other families is futile. Our children are already hurt and normal rules do not always apply. You are working towards building attachments and sometimes we just need to 'let it go' and move on.

Rules without Relationship lead to Rebellion.
Relationship without Rules leads to Chaos.
Relationship and Rules leads to Respect and
Responsibility.

Author unknown

RECOGNITION FOR BEING GOOD

If you want consequences to be effective, you also need to have rewards. If your child experiences all consequences and no rewards then life will feel punitive and this will damage your attachment with your child.

For example, the consequence for not getting home on time might be being grounded for a couple of days. But if your child comes home on time for five nights in a row, you could extend the time to be home a little later at the weekend. In other words, reward responsibility with greater trust.

If your child is furious with you for giving a consequence, remember that's the behaviour that got you here and stand firm. Do not back down. This could get ugly and you may both fall into old behaviour patterns; resist. If your child becomes violent again then step out of their way and wait for both parties to calm down before calmly telling your child that there is now another consequence. If you feel that your child is locked into a resistance/power struggle you may need external interventions to break the pattern. You could, perhaps, arrange an afternoon or sleepover with a respected member of your family or friends. You can also seek the support of a counsellor or a therapist (refer to Part Three for information on how to access counselling).

ATTACHMENT, EMPATHY, CONSCIENCE AND SELF-ESTEEM

If your adopted child has become locked into a determined pattern of destructive behaviour, this can be devastating for everyone. Perhaps your child has made a pact with their inner self that they will not love you and cannot lose face. In my case, it allowed me to feel I had some autonomy and power over my life when I was a child.

To bolster your relationship from this deterioration, encourage your adoptive child to develop their understanding of conscience and empathy – concepts that they may not have seen modelled in those around them previously. You can help your children develop a conscience by being attuned to them, not displaying violence or anger towards or in front of them and providing a secure, safe base for them, no matter what your own 'inner child' is telling you. Talk about situations that demonstrate a strong sense of right and wrong behaviour, and how we all take responsibility for our actions. Help them to experience positive outcomes from good behaviour and choices. We all make mistakes as parents, but openly admitting and apologising for these mistakes shows your child that you are human too.

To teach empathy you will need to help your child to think deeply about the potential effects of their actions on others. Examples around animals are a great way to instil this value with younger children. If your child hurts another child or one of your beloved pets, ask your child to say sorry. If the apology feels empty because your child doesn't understand what they have done, then keep talking. Ask the child how they think the person or animal felt after they hit them? Ask how the child felt when they inflicted the hurt and push them to give as much detail as possible. Explore these emotions and ask your child to explain back to you what those emotions are and what they feel like. Working through your child's tendency to use violence to show emotions will help you to forge a much stronger attachment, even if at the time you feel that your relationship is struggling.

If your child annoys or upsets you remember again that 'all behaviour is communication'. Your child is trying to talk to you. Yes, what they did was wrong but we are the adults and we need to help our child feel safe. Punishing or isolating your child just reinforces their fears and anxiety and this will sever the tender threads of attachment that you are striving to make. I have never seen any benefit by sending a child into confinement of any sort. Your child is craving your attention by their actions so give them positive attention as often as you can to encourage them to strive for and crave that good attention. Ignore your child at your peril, despite what some experts might say about not giving attention to bad behaviour. Your children need to learn about relationships in a positive manner so let them know you are there and care. (I have seen dramatic changes, with teenagers in particular, if you ignore traditional parenting models.)

Help your child find something they are good at and offer real praise for those achievements. False praise does little to enhance a real sense of self-esteem but acknowledging honest accomplishments and true ability helps build their self-confidence. Children given the opportunity to gain a sense of value by developing real skills and abilities show highly positive results.

As a child I didn't like myself. I had been told terribly cruel things and felt insecure in my unstable home environment. I cannot express enough how big these feelings are for a child to live with. Our job as parents is to help our children learn to love themselves before they can love us and others. By affirming their physical, mental and emotional attributes we show them they are loved and lovable. Thankfully, I found art. I worked hard to become good at it and this became a source of positive attention and praise that I had never received before. It was a life-changer.

RESTRAINT AND INTERVENTION

I don't think there is a feeling more overwhelming than knowing that your child wants to hurt you or themselves. Sadly we can't always rely on help at the speed we need it.

What looks like anger is a natural response for a young person when their heads and hearts are full of confusion and fear. You will know your child better than anyone and hopefully will recognise the early stages of a 'blow up'. If your child displays signs of agitation, irritation, anger or aggression, try to get in early before the temperature gets too hot to handle. I have learned to calmly distract the child with the most ridiculous ideas or comments. You may encourage some physical activity such as kicking or throwing a ball or taking the dog for a walk. My dogs have suffered near-exhaustion from our walks with one particular teenage boy who wanted to walk for miles and miles. He walked off his pain and I walked off the cake I had comfort-eaten to deal with the stress. If there is an adult or child who is prone to provoke them, keep them apart. Other children react better to activities that offer a sense of relaxation.

You may find yourself in a situation where you are holding a child against their will as they fight or threaten someone else. I have found, to my surprise, that if you hold them in a loose enough way so they can release themselves from you if they wish, that the child didn't want to be let go of. I believe they were looking for security from the safe adult. I have also held hands and put my arm round shoulders to divert a child away from dangerous situations. Remember our children probably have not experienced good parenting and learned safe boundaries. One child I looked after genuinely believed that hitting and kicking me was a way of expressing his love – his mum's boyfriend tormented him and beat him and his mum would say 'but he loves you'. We have no idea what has gone on before and we need to remember that while maintaining sanity and calm in our homes.

There are differing views about using restraint. Section 3(1) of the Criminal Law Act 1967 provides that 'a person may use such force as is reasonable in the circumstances in the prevention of a crime', meaning that you can use 'proportionate force' in order to protect yourself from another. Living with a violent child that you have committed to and love while everyone around you is offering their opinion is hard, very hard. I recommend that you start by seeking good restraint and de-escalation training. Ask your LA or adoption agency about this. Often they will 'buy in' a specialist who can train you to use safe techniques. (I have had to restrain children and young people and this should only be used as a last resort.) Most training assumes that there will always be two trained adults available to restrain a child but in reality this is not always the case so ask for advice around that. Learning restraining techniques will help your confidence and to some degree 'out' the problem in a sensible way.

* * *

Before I employ restraining techniques I might use myself as a presence. I will confidently stand in a doorway or in front of the person they are trying to take a swing at, making myself seem as large and solid as possible or I have often said distracting and daft things that has made the child laugh. This will swiftly change the mood. I see myself as a reminder and opportunity for the child or young person to make another choice. Sometimes they can't and, believe me, I understand it's hard when you feel out of control.

I once sat with a child who I initially thought wanted to kill me. I restrained him and within half an hour we were both giggling at the ridiculousness of our predicament. For me that was a far better method of restraining. Remember that material things can be replaced or mended and mean nothing compared to what your child and you are experiencing.

I cannot stress enough that your child does not 'hate' you. In fact you may be the only safe person or people in their life and that's why they can express themselves and push you to the brink . . .

CHAPTER 17:

Allegations and Complaints

When things go wrong it can feel like your world is collapsing around you and when an allegation is added into the mix it can feel like the end of the world. I want to remind you that the systems in place around allegations are not comfortable. Sadly too many allegations amount to nothing and if you go through this process it can have a damaging effect on everyone.

When I have supported parents through allegations I have been shocked at the mixed messages from the social worker or manager, and the lack of support. Unlike paid professionals, such as teachers or social workers, adopters have no rights or protection. Often an allegation leads to nothing, but the process will be distressing, and in some cases a child is removed, jobs and homes can be lost and lives turned upside down. A complaint against an adoptive parent can be malicious and mischievous – they can come from your child, their birth family or a social worker. It can cause insurmountable damage but mostly it can destroy trust. Trust is the most essential feeling that an adopted child and their adoptive parent can have.

I have known adopters receive an allegation from out of the blue. Some adopters have felt something brewing for a while. The simplest way to avoid getting involved in a potential allegation is to spot the warning signs that this might happen and act quickly. This may seem obvious but when life is busy it's easy not to notice the signs:

- Is your child displaying anger and trauma towards you?
- Does your child want to go back to their birth family? (They may have communicated on the internet and may be repeating conversations/situations to birth parents. Sometimes the birth parents can encourage a complaint about you.)
- Even if contact has been agreed by the courts, is it going well? (Or is your child finding it too much but can't articulate this because of split loyalties or fear.)

If a child has suggested to a teacher, social worker or someone else that you have done something bad to them that person is duty-bound to investigate. All children need to be heard, but it's not always that simple. A child might feel unhappy about a rule or expectation, or perhaps you raised your voice after you had asked your child for the fiftieth time to tidy their room. A child may have something going on that you do not even know about, and their fear or anger can be transferred onto you. Older children have access to the internet and can talk to their birth families so sometimes a destructive grip from inappropriate friends or family can influence your child's behaviour. Birth families who are angry with the LA for taking their child into care will see you as part of that fight. Your child may regret it as soon as they've done it but the process will start. Sometimes adopters are left wondering what has happened to them. It can be hard to come back from an allegation.

Allegations must be dealt with properly. The LA carries out the review, issuing you with an 'independent investigator' often known to the local authority or agency. Here are my top tips to protect yourself from an allegation:

- Usually there is a build-up to an allegation. If your child's behaviour begins to deteriorate, you need to keep a good written record of key events, concerns and issues, noting patterns of behaviour that become a theme.
- You should ensure this information is relayed by email to the social worker, which will capture the date and time. If you are not sending an email to someone else send it to yourself as a record.
- If you have done something, for example, taking the phone off your child and it dropped and smashed, you should photograph the phone and record the event. It is too easy for an incident like this to be blown out of proportion and misinterpreted. If you recognise potential problems, head them off.
- When noting the facts, be unemotional and concise in case you could be accused of being 'over emotional'. Note dates, times and locations. If your child has hurt themselves, download or draw a body map (a simple outline of the shape of the body with indicators of where an injury took place on their body). Photograph the injury with your phone camera and include a digital record of the date and time.
- Try not to become obsessed – keep yourself in a healthy place.

*We never thought an allegation could happen to us, we
had a wonderful relationship with our adopted son; we
should have paid more attention to his behaviour.
Because we were unprepared we went through a very
difficult time. Knowing what we know now we would
not let it get this out of our control again.*

David and Judy, adoptive parents

It is usually when an adoptive parent is at their most
exhausted and deflated that an allegation will appear. Try
to stay positive. It can be healthier for all parties to resolve
an allegation without involving solicitors. They will be
expensive and can close down channels of communication.
Mediation is cheaper and hopefully helps sustain working
relationships and, more importantly, protects the relationship with your child.

Confidentiality must be maintained at all times, so do
not email anyone not directly involved with the investigation. Keep your paperwork safe and lock it away.

Sometimes children have been removed from the family
home while an investigation is under way. I would urge you
to go through the social worker's paperwork in detail and if
you feel their comments do not reflect you, your child or
what has happened you are entitled to make corrections.
Sometimes there is an element of 'conversion' from what a
child has said to what is written and communicated by the
social worker. You can obtain all the data and information
the LA or agency has on you, including any records or
emails written about you by doing a Subject Access Request
(SAR). These are easy to do and local authorities must
adhere, by law, to the timeframes of a request.

MANAGING A COMPLAINT

Sometimes a relationship with your social worker or their manager breaks down, or you may have concerns about standards and practice. It can happen and it's really important that you deal with this professionally and reasonably.

When something has happened that upsets you or you are concerned about, try to avoid your email and phone for a little while and sleep on it. If you are troubled by your relationship with a professional keep up a 'let's work together' approach if at all possible. Ensure you keep records of your attempts; this is all about evidence, after all. You could use phrases such as 'as always we wish to work closely with the team around us to resolve this issue' or 'we are sure that you will agree with us that in the interests of the child' to demonstrate your efforts to work with the officials. Always try to smooth matters before you make an official complaint. I have found this difficult but it does look better if you try to sort out the issue first and, again, ensure your efforts are recorded in an email.

If you are going to make a complaint it should be professional and assertive but not aggressive. (If emotions get heated it could lead to a retaliatory allegation.) When you begin to write your complaint you need to refer to policy, protocol, National Minimum Standards and so on. Be clear where you think things could have gone better and calmly explain what you are concerned about. Be disciplined and clear; try to inspire an honest grown-up conversation that is focused on resolution and do not be tempted to take on the world. Any complaint should be about the breakdown of the joint working relationship rather than become personal or accusatory. You have a child who needs your energy and attention and that is always worth remembering.

Ensure also that your complaint is specific and targeted. Do not send hundreds of emails to different people within the organisation with different issues. Find out to whom you need to direct the email. Local authorities have steep hierarchical structures that they like to be used correctly. Start by sending it to one specific person with one other copied in. If you are not happy with the response you can escalate it up the chain then let them have time and space to come up with a response.

If you are making a complaint, be it informal or official, you should expect to be treated fairly. All is open to appeal and an official complaint will go to your Local Authority Designated Officer (LADO) and a judicial review after that. Nobody should be treated unfairly and all complaints should be treated as a positive opportunity to improve the service.

If you want to complain about a social worker after you feel that the response from their manager was not sufficient, you can contact Social Work England or the equivalent for your country. I would suggest that you call them first to see what information they require from you. Complaining about anything or anyone will require an evidence trail.

Again, you have a right to ask for personal data information, Subject Access Request (SAR), from the police or other groups who may be involved in your case. You will be able to check that your information is correct. If you are concerned about information recorded or given out about yourself you can contact the Information Commissioners Office (ICO), or look at their website. You are entitled to wait for this information throughout the investigation process. Do not feel pressured to forgo your findings since it is reasonable for you to gather evidence.

* * *

Most allegations stem from issues around behaviour. This is a huge and diverse area, and you and your child will have your own unique qualities and experiences. Remember all behaviour is communication. There is no 'right' way of being an adoptive parent and all our approaches will be different but I do strongly suggest that you attend training sessions held by your local authority or agency to help create an awareness of different approaches that may support your new family. None of us are experts, not even those who claim to be. As long as we are curious and keen to learn we will develop a pretty good understanding of what works for our child.

Because I have attended training I know how I need to behave while my child is doing their thing. We need to stay calm and de-escalate. We do not need to join in. Resist reacting in the moment, communicate well, be patient and take a deep breath. It's easier said than done but try not to take it personally.

If there is a behavioural incident you should record it – write your notes in a book and email them to yourself or your social worker. You are not being disloyal to your child, you are protecting your placement. If there is an allegation made against you later, you will be able to demonstrate a pattern and a build-up to the event.

CHAPTER 18:

How to Have Difficult Conversations

Over your time together, perhaps when you have been working together on the 'My Story' with your child or talking in the car about their birth parents or adding more photos in their memory box, you will be asked difficult questions or there will be opportunities that arise to discuss subjects that need to be raised. It is so important with adopted children that awkward subjects aren't glossed over and that they understand that you show them respect and trust with your honesty and empathy.

Talk to your child continually from early on in your relationship and ask them their views. Sometimes we yawn inside as we listen to their very long versions of inconsequential stories, but it's their story so they need to learn that they will be listened to. Before they go to bed get into the habit of asking them about their day or their feelings or practicalities about tomorrow. Ask their views on everything from the colour of your kitchen to how you should deal with a difficult (age-appropriate) situation. Keep the habit of talking in their lives. If they look like they don't want to engage, don't be offended – come back later. If these lines of communication close down, so will your relationship. It's the parents' job to twist and turn to find ways of reaching their children, but please don't expect or pressure your child to suddenly understand the importance of talking; it doesn't work like that.

I have listened to and read various approaches to giving difficult news to adopted children from social workers, therapists and other professionals.

I have some suggestions, not just based on theory but from listening to adopters, long-term foster carers, those who are special guardians or kinship carers and my own experiences of growing up in adoption and care. I was often left out of the loop and given bad news without any sensitivity or kindness. I am an adult who looks after other people's offspring who, on the whole, come with complicated, sometimes tragic pasts and in these situations the truth is the only thing that will do.

Think about your own childhood and how you received and felt about hearing sad or bad news. I don't know many families who haven't got or had secrets. These days I take the view that every child is different and children absorb information in different ways.

From my own experience of growing up in adoption and care, I see that young children below the age of four years will probably not make sense of most difficult news but you can still plant the seed. There is something protective about the feeling that 'I've always known', even if the child doesn't fully grasp the concept.

LANGUAGE

The language used in children's social care will make some of us roll our eyes and plead that they need to talk to the children in normal terms. Whether phrases like 'tummy mummies' or 'forever family' or 'happy hands', I find these phrases potentially dishonest – they will disable as many children as they help. We never know if a new family will be forever, and I have looked-after children who have lively hands that shake, rattle and roll as the child talks, but these hands can also be destructive and 'happy hands eat lovely food, happy hands catch a ball, happy hands hold a book to read' is too trite for most situations with a child who has been through trauma. I don't know where these phrases come from, but please send them back.

Comments can also bring more confusion and questions than answers. 'Mummy loved you very much' is an obvious favourite but this can stir confusion and sadness for the child. I remember asking myself that if she loved me very much, why am I here? In my experience of looking after children with trauma they're pretty sharp at understanding the difference between a platitude and genuine heartfelt support.

Looking through current advice from professionals on how to have 'difficult' conversations with children I am also struck by the way that language leans towards the child being the 'victim' and the adult as the 'rescuer'. I think this is a dangerous position to put children and adults into. A child does not need to feel like a victim. We've all heard the expression 'self-fulfilling prophecy' when others (adults) impose their own expectations and influence on a child's behaviour; the outcome will most likely reflect the ideas of the influential adult. I remember being at secondary school and stuck in a pattern of failure, missing school, bad attitude and so on. One teacher told me, 'Louise if you don't change you will end up on heroin and pregnant'. I did neither of these but I remember this expectation of me and what it said to me.

We want our children to grow up strong and confident. If you find yourself weeping into your coffee as you learn about your child's past then STOP. It's good to show empathy and understanding, but trust me when I say that your role is to provide a secure base as a sensitive and responsive attachment figure who meets the child's needs and to whom the child can turn as a safe haven when upset or anxious.

You will need to look after yourself during and after these conversations and altercations. As critical as I am of adults consciously or unconsciously imposing their views onto their children, I am aware that it can take some work to be aware that you are doing this.

BIRTH PARENTS WITH MENTAL HEALTH PROBLEMS

I grew up living with my adopted mother's mental health problems and she was often depressed or manic. Whether talking about bipolar disorder, severe depression or even schizophrenia, maybe 'Mummy/Daddy was not in control of their mind' will bring a little comfort. Remember that mental health disorders display in different ways and it's likely the child would have seen their parent act out a variety of different behaviours. It's good to talk about how this might have made them feel: 'it can be frightening living with an adult who has this illness because they can't look after you properly or keep you safe. That's why you live here with me'.

As your child grows older and their understanding develops you can sit with them and research mental health conditions online or in books. I recommend the NHS website for generic and balanced information. It is important that your child understands the characteristics of their parent's illness without shame. I prefer to be pragmatic about these issues and this avoids potential accusations of over-dramatising or not taking the issues seriously enough. Pitch it right in the middle.

BIRTH PARENTS WITH LEARNING DISABILITIES

Sometimes a child comes from a background where one or both parents have learning disabilities. The reality for a child living in those circumstances is two-fold. Ultimately, the care given to the child will likely have had limitations and could easily turn into neglect, and also other predatory adults can target parents with learning disabilities for easy access to vulnerable children. Remember we never know what really happened to our children.

It could be helpful to talk to your child about how 'babies and children need lots of love and attention and that there are a lot of things to remember but their mummy/daddy were not very good at remembering what she/he needed to do to keep you well and safe. They weren't able to learn these important skills to look after you so that's why you live here with me'.

DEATH

All children, adopted or not, will experience someone dying. The first thing we need to do is reassure the child that this happens to everyone sooner or later and it's totally normal. We will all die at some point from something. Depending on the child, and their relationship with you at the time, the conversation may cause different reactions. If your child doesn't react as you would expect, remember I talked earlier about not imposing your expectation onto your child. Their early life experience is different to yours.

I remember one of my children becoming obsessed with death; he searched for dead mini beasts to put in graves with elaborate decorations. This didn't bother me. I found it interesting and when he had thought about it enough his self-regulation kicked in and he moved on. If you feel that your child is becoming stuck in a deep investigation about the world, gently offer them a new one, for example, planets, kittens. All children I have looked after or worked with develop an obsession about something then drift away.

What if the death was a suicide? A child doesn't need to be in the care system to become aware of suicide; children like to discuss these matters at school and with friends. My children find subject matters like this deeply fascinating and I encourage discussion and debate so usually the subject has a shelf life. If it continues beyond a healthy timeframe then I begin to ask my young people who they are talking to and if they are looking on their phones at suicide sites. Just asking these questions can be enough to discourage them but sometimes you may need to do a gentle intervention.

Being open about death can be simple and effective and offer comfort to our children and us. It's also a good reason to ensure that the Life Story/My Story work is comprehensive so that those from their pre-adoption life are openly discussed if there is the possibility of a death in their birth family.

DRUGS AND ALCOHOL

It's not just children in the care system who are vulnerable to problems with alcohol and recreational drug-taking, it's all of us. We live in a stressful world that can feel unkind and pointless at times and it's important that we take the opportunity to let our children know that addiction is an illness, whether their birth parents had addiction problems or not. If your child lived with parents on drugs or alcohol, or both, the child will have experienced the deprivation, neglect and chaos that go with these addictions. Our children need to know that other people have these conditions, that these social problems go right across the social strata.

When you talk, you could discuss addiction and the symptoms of addition, chaotic lifestyles, poor money management, neglect and so on in the most appropriate way for your child. When you've had the conversation with your child, ask them to tell you what they have just learned. You will understand how much went in and how they have interpreted the information.

It is important that we do not demonise the birth parents for their addictions; often society has failed them. I have met birth parents who grew up in care and went on to have dysfunctional families that also resulted in their children entering the care system. I have distinct memories of how fine the line is for children and young people in care to become involved with negative destructive company and behaviour; they are vulnerable because no one 'has their back'.

HOW DO YOU FEEL ABOUT LEARNING THAT YOUR CHILD HAS SUFFERED SEXUAL ABUSE?

This is an important question as we don't know what has happened to our children. There may be evidence, even an investigation and arrest, you may begin to suspect that your child has been abused by their behaviour or they may disclose private details to you. I would suggest that if you are thinking of adopting a child that you need to ask yourself how you feel about this subject. I experienced sexual abuse as a child, from older children. It's hard for people to listen to and talk about. I decided to own it and take control rather than let it control me.

Growing up in care, fostered or adopted, you have files full of information about you, usually written by strangers and you can feel dehumanised just by that. Factor in child sexual abuse and you become something else again. As a younger woman, I overheard a group of men at a bar talking about a woman they knew, saying 'she'll be up for anything because she was abused as a child'. My stomach turned. The shame keeps us silent and so does not knowing how others will react.

Years ago I was sitting in a training session about child sexual abuse when I noticed that one of the other attendees kept squirming in his chair. He later got up and walked out, saying that he couldn't deal with it. He never came back.

Imagine how a child could feel watching an adult behave like this.

Looking after and living with a child who has experienced child sexual abuse is potentially part of what we do. We need to have accepted that this happened and remember it happened to the child not you. I strongly recommend you watch the TV drama *Three Girls*, based on the true stories of victims of grooming and sexual abuse in Rochdale to understand how it can happen to any child from any background, and the victim can be punished by ignorance and preconceptions.

* * *

Adopters must be open and honest from the beginning of the matching stage if they believe they will struggle with issues like this as they are likely to face big problems later in the child's life. If you are going to adopt a child you need to be emotionally available to your child.

CHAPTER 19:

What to Do if No One Seems to Be Listening

I would love to tell you that all communication channels and air waves will be open and available to you as an adopter, but I would be a big fat liar if I said that. There will be times of frustration when you feel that your ideas, concerns and wants fall on deaf ears.

Firstly – and this is important – know that you are not alone. It's one of the major complaints I hear from fellow adopters and foster carers, usually relating to up-and-coming court proceedings, contact, support or your child's mental health support. You know your child better than anyone and decisions can be made about your child by those who have never set eyes on them and that can feel emotional. Deep breath! We've all been there.

IT'S IN THE WAY WE SAY IT!

Not everyone who is adopting a child has a work history in the public sector and understands the 'ways' of the system. Some of us have little to no experience of the inner workings and logic of children's social care but it's an art that you need to master. To be heard, and to lower your blood pressure and smooth the way for better outcomes for you and your child, you need to speak 'their' language and work with the system:

Keep emotions in check: when a meeting is organised for the professionals to discuss your child and you are not invited it feels wrong on so many levels. You can feel unheard and rejected and, worse still for an adoptive parent, belittled as you're 'only' the parent. If this happens you will be in good company, which is why I strongly suggest you scream into your cushion, take a deep breath and start again with a pragmatic approach. Everything to do with adopting a child is emotional as it's all about relationships, but when it comes to dealing with the system and getting support for our children you need to be calm, business-like and efficient.

Choose your battles: by asking for support you find yourself and your child back in the system and, sadly, the culture can be unsupportive and leave you feeling you have been a bad parent. Steel yourself against any negative feedback you receive and save your energy for your child. Remember this is all about the child and working with the system to get the support you both need.

Ensure all information is available: before a meeting or email/letter regarding your child and any issues, you will need to have prepared your information. No one can predict the outcome of a professional's meeting but what you can do is deliver the best information to support awareness, actions and funding. Include the challenges and concerns you see every day for your child. Name these behaviours or issues, perhaps bedwetting, withdrawal or rages, and write a paragraph for each about how these behaviours impact your child and household.

Clearly state what you think could be prompting the problems: perhaps contact with the birth family or simply as a result of the trauma. Give examples of incidents or events that illustrate your point.

Submit your ideas for change: after you have clearly 'set out your stall' with the above information you can suggest some ideas that you feel could help improve the quality of your lives. This may be a suggestion to reduce or end contact. You may have researched a particular therapy that you feel could help your child. Suggest a few ideas for the issue; the professional team will need to decide what they think is best too. Now, they may 'put your child first' or the 'budget first', so be careful how you manage this. It will be a good idea to have researched what the outcomes will look like for your family. Factor in timescales and realistic goals and expectations. There is NO magic wand but different approaches may work with different children.

Set out next steps: decide with the professionals how and when you should report back on any improvements, or not. Again, you have not failed if your idea does not work straight away and professionals will know that. It may take several attempts to find a good solution to soothe your child's struggles.

Be flexible and be prepared to change your position: if you find resistance to your ideas and proposals please do not take it personally. If they suggest a different approach then agree to try it no matter what your inner voice is yelling. Ask for timelines and request your idea is reconsidered if this approach does not seem to work for your child. It's hugely frustrating, but be patient.

Avoid conflict: remain professional or you will end up feeling that you are 'just the parent' and that's not how any of us needs to feel.

As someone who has not always felt cool and calm in these meetings, especially when hearing the polar opposite to my informed knowledge and ideas for my child, I cannot stress enough how important it is that you remain polite, cool and calm.

You need the professionals to have confidence in you. There will be no doubt that you love your child but, ironically, during these meetings that will not get you what you want. Keep in mind that the meetings are about your child not you, but you and your household matter too.

RESPITE

The Department for Education's Adoption Minimum Standards sadly do not include respite for adopters but I think that respite is a major underused solution – short-term, or on a regular basis.

Respite could be the solution to prevent 'blocked care' or simply when the adopter needs a break from the child or young person whose behaviour is making them feel depressed and exhausted. I have struggled with social workers' and their managers' attitudes to adopters needing a break. I genuinely don't understand why they are so judgemental and reluctant to support the idea. Taking a break is not failure; staying in a toxic situation is failure. Removing yourself from it to rest and feel better, that's a success.

Looking after children who have experienced trauma can feel like a tough job but in even the harshest jobs, you can take a break, that's normal. Personally I think all social workers and associated professionals should experience looking after children with trauma. Often the theory of childcare falls short of being effective in ongoing real-life scenarios.

If you feel strongly that a break or regular breaks would help save the relationship with your child then please 'stamp your feet'. If your request for respite is rejected, I would recommend you take that up with your social worker and their manager and appeal.

Finding someone to look after your child can be a challenge; if friends and family have seen your child on their worst day, offers may dwindle. Foster care would be the obvious solution but the legal framework is not set up for that and your child would have to become a looked-after child to be fostered, even just for respite. This rule needs to be changed if the 'system' wants to help prevent adoption disruptions.

TRUSTING YOURSELF

I make plenty of mistakes and I am impressed by my children's ability to forgive them (only after mocking me first or stomping off, of course). Society expects so much from us, as do we ourselves. We can be overly self-critical and because we have adopted a child there are many other layers of doubt and analysis.

Sometimes you will feel overwhelmed and that's normal. It's not a sign of weakness, it's a way of reminding yourself to do this differently. Firstly, you are not going to be the best parent if you're tired – I'm hopeless and grumpy if I haven't had enough sleep. Wait to deal with whatever has come up, if possible. Take your time and slow down. Sometimes by the time we feel physically and emotionally ready to deal with a child's situation it may seem less relevant. It's not a competition to attend to every detail of your child's life, sometimes sitting down with a cup of tea and the remote control is good enough!

Our children are the vehicles to our change. They shape our lives with their interests, enthusiasm and freshness. They may have a history that will make us think, feel and see the world differently. Their energy can invigorate us. I asked a GP once what the best way was to stave off old age, and he said with a smile, 'Children'.

I could not resist quoting the legendary Dr Spock:

'Trust yourself, you know more than you think.'

FINAL NOTE

Well done!

You made it through to the end of my book, and now I hope you feel ready to begin your exciting adoption journey.

Be aware that adoption does not work for all children or all adopters. There are many variables – from your child not recognising the love you are ready to give or perhaps you are still grieving the unsuccessful and expensive IVF that has helped bring you to adoption but you're not quite in the right space yet. I believe the key to a good-quality adoption is the initial work you do on yourself. To know yourself as honestly as you can will help your child understand and learn who you are too. How will a child from another background 'get you' if you're still not sure who you are?

Everything about adoption is courageous, brave and unimaginably emotional. I still cry just thinking about someone deciding to adopt a child as I think it's one of the most amazing things we can do. There are many flaws in the adoption system that I wish I could change but I can't – but what I can do is prepare you for what the rest of us had to work out for ourselves.

I need to tell you that even on your hardest day, and there will hard days, that you have done something so beautiful. Every child deserves the opportunity to be loved and to feel loved.

NO EXCUSES

There are no excuses for child abuse and neglect.

There are no excuses for why a child is experiencing trauma.

Trauma shows itself both loudly and quietly, sometimes you would never know it was there.

And no adult who has experienced that trauma should feel that is okay to pass it on.

A bad childhood is not an excuse.

Those who have influence, power and profession, you have no excuse to allow it to continue.

The ones who choose to abuse and neglect children, you have no excuse.

There are no excuses for the way we treat some of our children.

I write my books for those children, whether still young or grown, who know things that others don't and hopefully never will.

ADOPTION ACRONYMS AND TERMS

ACA-SF Assessment Checklist for Adolescents (Short Form)

ACE Alternative Complementary Education

ACEs Adverse Childhood Experiences

ADD Attention Deficit Disorder

ADHD Attention Deficit Hyperactivity Disorder

ADM Agency Decision-maker

Adoption Order An adoption order grants complete parental responsibility to the new parents and severs the tie with birth parents

Adoptive Placement The point at which a child begins to live with prospective adoptive parents; the period before the adoption is finalised

AFCARS Adoption and Foster Care Analysis and Reporting System

AP Alternative Provision (for children not in mainstream school)/Advanced Practitioner

ARC/LAC Panel Panel for children's and young people's cases who are 'At Risk of Care'/'Looked-after'

ASC Autism Spectrum Condition/Adult Social Care

ASD Autism Spectrum Disorder

ASF Adoption Support Fund set up by the government to pay for therapeutic services including therapeutic parenting training and intensive family interventions

ASP Adoption Support Plan

BAAF CoramBAAF Adoption and Fostering Academy (formerly British Association for Adoption and Fostering)

BASE Barnardo's Against Sexual Exploitation

BESD Behavioural, emotional and social difficulties

BSL British Sign Language

C&I Communication and interaction

C&L Cognition and learning

C&YP Children and Young People

CAF Common Assessment Framework

CAIT/CAIU Child Abuse Investigation Team/Unit (Police)

CAMAT Child Abuse Multi-Agency Training

CAMHS Child and Adolescent Mental Health Services (now CYPMHS) – referral can be through your GP, social worker or school

CANS Children with Additional Needs Support

CARA Cautions and Relationship Abuse Scheme/Children At Risk Assessment

Care Act 2014 Requires local authorities to help develop a market that delivers a wide range of sustainable high-quality care and support services that will be available to their communities

CareFirst Social Care information system/database recording key information about children and young people, including any assessments and placement addresses

Care Plan All children in care are required to have a Care Plan (completed by the social worker) which sets out how the child or young person's needs are to be met, including care, education and health arrangements

CBT Cognitive Behaviour Therapy

CC Children's Centre

CCG Clinical Commissioning Group

CDC Child Development Centre

CE Child Exploitation

CEIAG Careers Education, Information, Advice and Guidance

CEOP Child Exploitation and Online Protection Centre (tackling child sex abuse and providing advice)

CHC Continuing Healthcare

CiC Children in Care/Looked-after children

CIN Children in Need

CLA Child Looked After

CLD Complex Learning Difficulties

CME Children Missing Education

Contact Contact between a child and another person or persons including the child's parents, as defined in Section 34 of the Children Act

CP Child Protection

CPD Continuous Professional Development

CP-IS Child Protection Information Sharing project

CPOMS Child Protection Online Monitoring and Safeguarding system (safeguarding and child protection software for schools)

CPR Child Permanence Report

CPSU Child Protection in Sport Unit

CQC Care Quality Commission

CRB checks Criminal Records Bureau checks (now DBS checks)

CRCs Community Rehabilitation Companies

CRP Children's Resource Panel – a meeting to consider the resources needed by children and young people either in or on the edge of care

CSA Child Sexual Abuse

CSC Children's Social Care

CSE Child Sexual Exploitation

CSIB Children's Services Improvement Board

CSW Children's Social Worker

CVAA Consortium of Voluntary Adoption Agencies

CYP&F Children, Young People and Families Service

CYPMHS Children and Young People's Mental Health Services

DA Domestic Abuse

DASH Domestic Abuse, Stalking and Harassment and Honour-based Violence

DASV Domestic Abuse and Sexual Violence

DBS Disclosure and Barring Service (England and Wales)

DCPO Designated Child Protection Officer – the member of staff coordinating child safeguarding concerns and making referrals

DfE Department for Education

DoLS Deprivation of Liberty Safeguards/Liberty Protection Safeguards under the Mental Capacity Act

DSL Designated Safeguarding Lead

DV Domestic violence

DVPN Domestic Violence Protection Notice – served by the police against an adult, where the police reasonably believe that they have been violent or have threatened violence against an individual who needs to be protected

DVPN/DVPO Domestic Violence Prevention Notice/Order – once a DVPN is served, it must be presented to a magistrates' court for approval

DWP Department of Work and Pensions

Early Help/Early Intervention Action to support a child, young person of family as soon as a problem is identified

Early Years A phrase used to describe the initial years of a
child's life

ECIP Emergency Care Improvement Programme

EET Education, Employment and Training

EfC Employers for Carers

EH&TS offer Early Help and Targeted Support offer

EHAT Early Help Assessment Tool

EHC Education, Health and Care

EHCP/HCP Education, Health and Care Plan

EHE Elective Home Education

EHWB Emotional Health and Wellbeing

EOTAS Education Other Than School

EP Educational Psychologist

EP&S Education, Participation and Skills

EPO Emergency Protection Order

EPP Early Permanence Plan

EPS Educational Psychology Service

ESFA Education and Skills Funding Agency

ESG Education Services Grant

ESOL English for Speakers of Other Languages

Expressive Communication The ability to express
thoughts, feelings and needs verbally (using words and
sentences) and non-verbally (for example, using gestures,
facial expressions, gaze, signing and other methods that
supplement or replace speech or writing)

EWO Education Welfare Officer

EYFS Early Years Foundation Stage

FASB Fair Access to Short Breaks

FASD Foetal Alcohol Spectrum Disorder

FASS Family Assessment and Safeguarding Service

FAQ Frequently Asked Questions

FC Foster Carer/Foster Child

FE Further Education

FFT Functional Family Therapy

FGC Family Group Conference

FGM Female Genital Mutilation

FII Fabricated or Induced Illness

FIP Family Intervention Project

FIS Family Information Service

FMU Forced Marriage Unit

FNP Family Nurse Partnership

FTE Full-time equivalent

FWAF Families with a Future

GBH Grievous Bodily Harm

GM Genital Mutilation

GP General Practitioner (doctor)

Guardian Ad Litem – Court-appointed guardian independent of birth family and social services who represents the child's interests

HBV Honour-based Violence

HCPC Health and Care Professions Council. An independent regulatory body responsible for setting and maintaining standards of training, performance and conduct of healthcare professions

High Needs Funding Intended to provide the most appropriate support package for an individual with special educational needs and disabilities

HR Healthy Relationships/Human Resources

HSB Harmful Sexual Behaviour

HSCT Health and Social Care Trust

IA Information and Advice

IAA Independent Adoption Agency

IAG Information, advice and guidance

IAPT Improving Access to Psychological Therapies

IAW In accordance with

IAW Team Inclusion, Attendance and Welfare Team

ICS Integrated Children's Services/System

IEP Individual Education Plan

IFA Independent Fostering Agency – private fostering services commissioned by the Local Authority

IFPS Intensive Family Preservation Services

In-House Foster Care Foster carers recruited by the Local Authority

IHWB Integrated Health and Well-being

ILACS Inspection of Local Authority Children's Services

IMR Internal Management Review/Independent Management Review

Inter-Agency working More than one agency working together in a planned and formal way

IRO Independent Reviewing Officer

IRL 'In Real Life' as opposed to online

ISA Independent Safeguarding Authority

ISC Independent Schools Council

ISI Independent Schools Inspectorate

ITT Independent Travel Training

Joined-up Deliberate and coordinated planning and working which takes account of different policies and varying agency practice and values

Joint Funding Panel A panel consisting of Social Care, Education and Health representatives who meet to consider shared funding arrangements for placements for children and young people with complex additional needs, usually children with EHCPs and/or complex health needs

Joint Working Professionals from more than one agency working directly together on a project

JSNA Joint Strategic Needs Assessment

JTAI Joint Targeted Area Inspection

KCSiE Keeping Children Safe in Education

KS1 Key Stage 1 (School years: Reception, Y1, Y2)

KS2 Key Stage 2 (School years: Y3, Y4, Y5, Y6)

KS3 Key Stage 3 (School years: Y7, Y8, Y9)

KS4 Key Stage 4 (School years: Y10, Y11)

LA Local Authority

LAC Looked-after Children

LC Learning Community

LCP Local Care Partnership

LD Learning Disability

LDA Learning Disability Assessment

LDP Learning Disability Partnership

LEP Local Education Partnership/Local Enterprise Partnership

LGO Local Government Ombudsman

LP Lead Professional

LSA Learning Support Assistant

LSCB Local Safeguarding Children Board

LSP Local Safeguarding Partnership

MAPPA Multi-Agency Public Protection Arrangement

MARAC Multi-Agency Risk Assessment Conference

MASH Multi-Agency Safeguarding Hub

MAST Multi-Agency Support Team

MCA Mental Capacity Act

MEAM Making Every Adult Matter

MEYSOG Maternity and Early Years System Optimisation Group

MFM Mockingbird Family Model – sometimes used by local authorities to enable families to receive non-judgemental support

MH Mental Health

MHCLG Ministry of Housing, Communities and Local Government

MLD Moderate Learning Difficulties

MSI Multi-Sensory Impairment

MST Multi-Sensory Therapy

MST-CAN Multi-Systemic Therapy for Child Abuse and Neglect

Multi-Agency/cross-agency working More than one agency working together and pooling budgets and resources

Multi-Professional/multi-disciplinary working Staff with different professional backgrounds and training working together

NEET Not in Education, Employment or Training

Networks Informal contact and communication between individuals and agencies

NHS National Health Service

NICE National Institute for Health and Care Excellence

NMS National Minimum Standards

NPS National Probation Service

NQT Newly Qualified Teacher

OCD Obsessive-Compulsive Disorder

Ofsted Office for Standards in Education, Children's Services and Skills – reports directly to Parliament and is both independent and impartial. By law it must inspect schools with the aim of providing information to parents, to promote improvement and to hold schools to account

ONS Office for National Statistics

OPCC Office of the Police and Crime Commissioner

OPG Office of the Public Guardian

OSOA One System One Aim

OT Occupational Therapist/Therapy

PACE 'Playfulness, acceptance, curiosity and empathy'. PACE is a way of thinking, feeling, communicating and behaving that aims to make the child feel safe. It is based upon how parents connect with their very young infants. As with young toddlers, with safety the child can begin to explore

PAR Prospective Adopter Report

PASM Professional Allegations Strategy Meeting

Pathway Plan All young people over 16 in care are required to have a Pathway Plan which sets out the actions for their progress towards adulthood

PD Physical Disability

PDG Project Delivery Group

PEP Personal Education Plan

PfA Preparing for Adulthood

Placement Plan All children in care have a Placement Plan completed before their placement begins (or within five working days) which states the requirements of the placement in meeting the needs of the child or young person

PMLD Profound and Multiple Learning Disabilities

PNC record Police National Computer record

PoCA Protection of Children Act 1989

PoCSA Protection of Children (Scotland) Act 2003

PPM Placement Planning Meeting

PPS Parent Partnership Service

PR Parental Responsibility – automatically assigned to all birth mothers (and to fathers named and present at issue of the birth certificate). Fathers not present have to apply to the courts. A child in care may either be 'Accommodated' (parents retain PR) or on a Care Order/Interim Care Order/Residence Order/Special Guardianship (Local Authority/other shares PR).

PRU Pupil Referral Unit

PSP Primary Support Provider

PTSD Post-Traumatic Stress Disorder

PUP Parents Under Pressure (parenting programme)

Pupil Premium Additional funding to raise the attainment of disadvantaged pupils of all abilities and to close the gaps between them and their peers

PVG Protection of Vulnerable Groups scheme

PVI Private voluntary and independent

P16 Post-16

RAA Regional Adoption Agency

RAD Reactive Attachment Disorder

RAM Resource Allocation Model

REACH The missing young person and exploitation practitioners who complete return home interviews

Reactive strategy Strategy used to make a situation or a person safe when they behave in a challenging way

Receptive communication Ability to understand or comprehend language (either spoken or written) or other means of communication

Registered Manager Manager of children's home, responsible for the day-to-day operation of the home

Residential Order When parents are separating, divorcing or applying for civil partnership dissolution and can't agree on arrangements for their children, they can turn to the courts for help. The family courts can issue a contact or residence order that will determine visiting rights and where the child will live

Restrictive interventions Interventions that may infringe a person's human rights and freedom of movement, including locking doors, preventing a person from entering certain areas of the living space, seclusion, manual and mechanical restraint, rapid tranquilisation and long-term sedation

RI Responsible Individual acts on behalf of a children's home provider to ensure that the legal responsibilities are carried out and is accountable for ensuring the effectiveness of the Registered Manager and the quality of the care

RO Residence Order

RSC Regional Schools Commissioner

RTT Referral to Treatment Time

SAB Safeguarding Adults Board

SAR Safeguarding Adults Review

SCB Safeguarding Children Board

SCR Serious Case Review

SDQ Strengths and Difficulties Questionnaire – a brief behavioural screening questionnaire about three- to sixteen- year olds

Section 17 of the Children Act 1989 gives local authorities a general duty to safeguard and promote the welfare of children within their area who are in need

Section 20 of the Children Act 1989 states that the local authority has a duty to provide a child with somewhere to live if the child doesn't have a home or has a home which is deemed unsafe

Section 47 of the Children Act 1989 places a duty on local authorities to make enquiries into the circumstances of children considered to be at risk of significant harm and, where these inquiries indicate the need, to decide what action, if any, it may need to take to safeguard and promote the child's welfare

Section 47 Enquiry Initiated if a child is taken into police protection, is the subject of an Emergency Protection Order, or there are reasonable grounds to suspect that a child is suffering or is likely to suffer significant harm

SIAMS Statutory Inspection of Anglican and Methodist Schools – evaluates the distinctiveness and effectiveness of the school as a church school, and how well the distinctive Christian character and ethos of the school ensure the development and achievement of the whole child or young person

SoS Signs of Safety

Sxtortion/sextortion A form of sexual exploitation involving blackmail, extortion and/or bullying of a victim by a perpetrator who possesses sexual images/video of them

SW Social Worker

SSW Supervising or Senior Social Worker/Social Service Worker

SWE Social Work England, a new organisation that took over from HCPC (Health Care Professionals Council)

covering all social worker membership. You can make formal complaints against individual social workers

T&F Task and Finish Group

TAC Team Around the Child

TAF Team Around the Family

TAM Team Around Me

Targeted interventions Offer specific support for those children and young people who are felt to be vulnerable in relation to speech, language and communication

TF Troubled Families (programme)

TfC Together for Childhood

TS Targeted Support

Treatment manual Detailed advice and guidance on how to deliver an intervention, including its content, duration and frequency

Universal interventions Support the whole population, i.e. whole class or whole setting/school and ensure all children have appropriate language and communication opportunities

UPN Unique Pupil Number

VAA Voluntary Adoption Agency

VAWG Violence against Women and Girls

VCS Voluntary and Community Sector

ViST Vulnerability Screening Tool

VS Virtual School

VSH Virtual School Head

UKCCIS UK Council for Child Internet Safety

WTSC Working Together to Safeguard Children

YOI Young Offender Institute
YOT Youth Offending Team
YP Young People

USEFUL ORGANISATIONS AND SUPPORT

GENERAL

Action for Children (formerly National Children's Homes NCH)

Provides Adoption support across England, Wales, Scotland and Northern Ireland.

Website: www.actionforchildren.org.uk

Email: ask.us@actionforchildren.org.uk

Adopters for Adoption

Agency (England only) looking to have a positive impact on how adopters are supported in the adoption process.

Website: www.adoptersforadoption.com

Email: contactus@adoptersforadoption.com

Adoption UK

Adoption UK is the leading charity providing support, community and advocacy for all those parenting or supporting children who cannot live with their birth parents, covering England, Wales, Scotland and Northern Ireland. Very helpful resources and webinars on a range of subjects and arranges regional meet-ups/groups. Includes helpful forum for disabled adopters.

Website: www.adoptionuk.org

Email: info@adoptionuk.org.uk

Barnardo's

Dedicated adoption support services specialising in post-adoption support across the UK, and helping others who are affected by adoption including birth families and adopted adults. Barnardo's BASE (Barnardo's Against Sexual Exploitation) campaign is a series of regional groups supporting children at risk of sexual exploitation.

Website: www.barnardos.org.uk

Email: makingconnections@barnardos.org.uk

Carers Trust

Charity for, with and about unpaid carers. The charity gives carers a voice and highlights their work to the general public. It also campaigns and works with politicians and policy holders to create real change for unpaid carers throughout the UK.

Website: www.carers.org

Email: info@carers.org

Consortium of Voluntary Adoption Agencies

Membership organisations for VAAs across all of the UK. Visit its website to find an agency near you. They also have a helpful listing of all relevant legislation around adoption for all countries in the UK.

Website: www.cvaa.org.uk

CoramBAAF

CoramBAAF is an independent membership organisation for professionals, foster carers and adopters, and anyone else working with or looking after children in or from care, or adults who have been affected by adoption. It is a successor organisation to the British Association for Adoption and Fostering (BAAF).
Website: www.corambaaf.org.uk

First4adoption

First4Adoption is the national information service for people interested in adopting a child in England. It gives clear and impartial information about adopting and can put you in touch with adoption agencies in your area.
Website: www.first4adoption.org.uk

Netmums

Advice for all things parenting, including comprehensive online forum.
Website: www.netmums.com

NSPCC

Call the free NSPCC helpline on 0808 800 5000 or report any childcare/safeguarding concerns online.
Website: www.nspcc.org.uk
Email: help@nspcc.org.uk

Social Work England

Regulatory organisation covering all social worker membership. You can raise a concern or formal complaint against social workers with this organisation.
Website: www.socialworkengland.org.uk

ADOPTION AGENCIES – ENGLAND

Northern England

Adoption Matters
Large VAA providing a range of support, including intermediary services, across northern England and parts of Wales and the Midlands.
Website: www.adoptionmatters.org
Email: info@adoptionmatters.org

Adopt North East
RAA covering Northumberland, Newcastle, North Tyneside, South Tyneside and Gateshead.
Website: www.adoptnortheast.org.uk
Email: adoptnortheast@northtyneside.gov.uk

Adoption NoW
Agency in the north-west of England covering Rochdale, Oldham, Tameside, Bury, Bolton and Blackburn with Darwen.
Website: www.adoptionnow.org.uk

Adoption Tees Valley
RAA covering the north-east of England and the five LAs of Middlesbrough, Stockton, Hartlepool, Redcar and Cleveland and Darlington.
Website: www.adoptionteesvalley.org.uk
Email: info@adoptionteesvalley.org.uk

Arc Adoption North East

Independent voluntary adoption agency (VAA) located in the north-east of England.

Website: www.arcadoptionne.org.uk

Email: info@arcadoptionne.org.uk

Caritas Care

Independent adoption agency covering the whole of the north-west of England including Lancashire, Greater Manchester, Cumbria and parts of Yorkshire, as well as parts of Scotland including the Dumfries area.

Website: www.caritascare.org.uk

Email: info@caritascare.org.uk

Together for Children

Delivers adoption services for Sunderland City Council.

Website: www.togetherforchildren.org.uk

Email: adoption@togetherforchildren.org.uk

Central England

Adoption@heart

RAA covering Wolverhampton, Walsall, Dudley and Sandwell Children's Trust.

Website: www.adoptionatheart.org.uk

Email: info@adoptionatheart.org.uk

Adoption Central England (ACE)

RAA covering Worcestershire, Warwickshire, Solihull, Coventry and Herefordshire.

Website: www.aceadoption.com

Email: enquiries@aceadoption.com

Adoption Connects
RAA covering Milton Keynes and Central Bedfordshire.
Website: www.adoptionconnects.co.uk
Email: enquiries@adoptionconnects.co.uk

Adoption Counts
RAA covering Salford, Trafford, Manchester, Stockport and Cheshire East.
Website: www.adoptioncounts.org.uk
Email: adoptionenquiries@adoptioncounts.org.uk

Adoption East Midlands
Organisation comprising VAAs and RAAs covering Derbyshire, Derby, Nottinghamshire and Nottingham.
Website: www.adoptioneastmidlands.org.uk
Email: enquiries@adoptioneastmidlands.nottscc.gov.uk

Adoption Focus
Agency offering a range of services across Birmingham, Staffordshire and Oxfordshire, including training and support groups.
Website: www.adoption-focus.org.uk
Email: enquiries@triangleproject.org.uk

Adoption in Merseyside (AiM)
A regional adoption agency that covers the four local authorities, Liverpool, Sefton, Knowsley and Wirral.
Website: www.adoptioninmerseyside.co.uk

AdoptionPlus

Adoption agency based in Milton Keynes, Buckinghamshire, offering an adoption placement service, specialist adoption therapy services, training and conferences.
Website: www.adoptionplus.co.uk
Email: enquiries@adoptionplus.co.uk

Adoption West

RAA covering Gloucestershire, South Gloucestershire, Wiltshire, Bristol, North Somerset and Bath and north-east Somerset
Website: www.adoptionwest.co.uk

Birmingham Children's Trust

A trust covering the Birmingham area.
Website: www.birminghamchildrenstrust.co.uk

CCS Adoption

Independent adoption agency in Bristol, working across the Adoption West region in Bristol, South Gloucestershire, Gloucestershire, Somerset, Bath and north-east Somerset, north Somerset, Swindon, Wiltshire and South Wales.
Website: www.ccsadoption.org
Email: info@ccsadoption.org

Faith in Families

Independent adoption and adoption support agency working throughout the East Midlands, including therapeutic support, training and support groups.
Website: www.faithinfamilies.org
Email: enquiries@faithinfamilies.org
0115 955 8811

Together for Adoption

RAA covering Cheshire West and Chester, Halton, Warrington, St Helens and Wigan.

Website: www.togetherforadoption.co.uk

London and Southern England

Adopt East

RAA working with families in Southend, Thurrock, Essex, Suffolk, Norfolk, Hertfordshire, Bedford and Luton. Refer to website to contact your local agency.

Website: www.adopteast.org.uk

Adopt London

Group of four RAAs covering 23 London LAs: Adopt London East, Adopt London West, Adopt London North, Adopt London West.

Website: www.adoptlondon.org.uk

Adopt South

RAA covering Hampshire County, Isle of Wight, Portsmouth and Southampton.

Website: www.hants.gov.uk/socialcareandhealth/adoptsouth

Adoption South East

RAA comprising Brighton and Hove, East Sussex, Surrey and West Sussex.

Website: www.adoptionsoutheast.org.uk

Adopt South West
RAA covering Devon, Somerset, Plymouth and Torbay.
Website: www.adoptsouthwest.org.uk
Email: adoptsouthwest@devon.gov.uk

Aspire Adoption Services
RAA covering Dorset, Bournemouth, Poole and Christchurch.
Website: www.aspireadoption.co.uk
Email: enquiries@aspireadoption.co.uk

Coram Ambitious for Adoption
Independent adoption agency working across Greater London and the surrounding areas, as well as the East Midlands.
Website: www.coramadoption.org.uk
Email: adoption@coram.org.uk

Diagrama Foundation
Independent VAA finding families able to offer a permanent home for children in need of adoption across south London, Surrey, East and West Sussex, Berkshire, Kent and Hampshire.
Website: www.diagramaadoption.org.uk
Email: adoption@diagrama.org.uk

Families For Children
Independent adoption agency covering the south-west of England.
Website: www.familiesforchildren.org.uk
Email: info@familiesforchildren.org.uk

Family Futures

An independent adoption and fostering agency, providing assessment and therapy for children who have experienced trauma and support for their families.

Website: www.familyfutures.co.uk

Email: contact@familyfutures.co.uk

Parents and Children Together (PACT)

Adoption charity and VAA provider of adoption services, therapeutic support and community projects across London and the south of England.

Website: www.pactcharity.org

Slough Children's Services Trust

Provides support and social care services for children, young people and families in Slough.

Website: www.scstrust.co.uk

Email: emailus@scstrust.co.uk

SCOTLAND ADOPTION SUPPORT

Adopting a Child in Scotland

General adoption information for Scotland and postcode search to find your nearest agency.

Website: www.mygov.scot/adopting-child-scotland

Birthlink (Adults affected by adoption)

Birthlink aims to enhance the wellbeing and promote the welfare of those with a Scottish connection affected by adoption.

Website: www.birthlink.org.uk

Email: mail@birthlink.org.uk

Scotland's Adoption Register

Scottish government project supporting the family-finding process in Scotland. Find your local Scottish agencies using the website's map search option.

Website: www.scotlandsadoptionregister.org.uk

Email: sar@adoptionregister.scot

Scottish Adoption

An organisation delivering high-quality, innovative services to all affected by adoption in Scotland and further afield.

Website: www.scottishadoption.org

Email: info@scottishadoption.org

NORTHERN IRELAND ADOPTION SUPPORT

Adopt NI

An independent registered charity established to support any adult impacted by the lifelong journey of adoption. Based in Belfast but working on a regional basis, it also deals frequently with enquiries from people in Ireland, mainland UK and from other countries like Australia and America where people have a link to Northern Ireland.

Website: www.adoptni.org

Email: info@adoptni.org

Family Care Adoption

Family Care Adoption is the largest specialist Adoption Agency in Northern Ireland, with offices in Belfast and Derry.

Website: www.familycareadoption.com

HSC Northern Ireland Adoption and Foster Care

The largest recruitment service for adoption and foster care across Northern Ireland. The five Health and Social Care Trusts have statutory responsibility for all children and young people who require an adoptive family or foster carers.
Website: www.adoptionandfostercare.hscni.net

WALES ADOPTION SUPPORT

Adoption Mid and West Wales

Regional adoption service for Carmarthenshire, Ceredigion, Pembrokeshire and Powys.
Website: www.adoptionmwwales.org.uk
Email: adoptionenquiries@carmarthenshire.gov.uk

National Adoption Service Wales

Supports best practice in adoption across Wales, including search option for local agencies.
Website: www.adoptcymru.com

North Wales Adoption Service

Covering Wrexham, Flintshire, Denbighshire, Conwy, Gwynedd and Ynys Mon.
Website: www.northwalesadoption.gov.uk

St David's Children Society

Locally based adoption support services across Wales.
Website: www.adoptionwales.org
Email: info@stdavidscs.org

South East Wales Adoption Service

Covering Blaenau Gwent, Caerphilly, Monmouthshire, Newport and Torfaen.
Website: www.southeastwalesadoption.co.uk

Vale, Valleys and Cardiff Adoption

Covering Merthyr Tydfil, Rhondda Cynon Taff, Cardiff Council or the Vale of Glamorgan.
Website: www.valeofglamorgan.gov.uk

Western Bay Adoption Service

Covering Bridgend, Neath Port Talbot and Swansea areas.
Website: www.westernbayadoption.org

ADOPTER SUPPORT ORGANISATIONS

Gingerbread

Charity supporting and campaigning for single parent families across England and Wales, including an online forum and local groups.
Website: www.gingerbread.org.uk

Intercountry Adoption Centre (IAC)

Agency providing a comprehensive service to people considering both domestic and intercountry adoption. The agency also caters to adopted adults, birth relatives and to professionals working in the intercountry field.
Website: www.icacentre.org.uk

New Family Social

Support charity for LGBT+ families, adopters and foster carers, including a social network and working with agencies across the UK.

Website: www.newfamilysocial.org.uk

SSAFA (the Armed Forces charity)

Charity providing adoption services suitable for members of the armed forces.

Website: www.ssafa.org.uk

GENERAL SUPPORT

Beacon House

A specialist, innovative and creative therapeutic service for young people, families and adults, with a special interest in working with individuals of all ages who have experienced trauma and loss. Clinics in Cuckfield and Chichester.

Website: www.beaconhouse.org.uk

Email: admin@beaconhouse.org.uk

Become

Works to improve the everyday lives and future life chances of children in care and young care-leavers through training for organisations working with LAC, plus free life coaching programme for care-leavers. Care advice line freephone 0800 023 2033.

Website: www.becomecharity.org.uk

Email: advice@becomecharity.org.uk

Buttle.org/Chances for Children

Grant programme run by charity dedicated to helping children and young people in crisis reach their potential, from finance for small household items to larger educational needs.

Website: www.buttleuk.org

Catholic Children's Society (Westminster)

Specialises in post-adoption support, counselling and training through schools, and also provides tracing and intermediary services for adults who were once in their care.

Website: www.cathchild.org.uk

Email: info@cathchild.org.uk

Child Psychology Service

Midlands-based clinical psychology service for children. Can assess for a variety of problems including ADHD, Anxiety, Depression, Attachment Disorder, Conduct Disorder, grief and bereavement and trauma (including Post Traumatic Stress Disorder).

Website: www.thechildpsychologyservice.co.uk

Email: enquiries@thechildpsychologyservice.co.uk

DDP network

Dyadic Developmental Psychotherapy (DDP) (based on attachment theory, and the neurobiology of trauma, attachment and caregiving). Provides training and events for parents, carers and professionals.

Website: www.ddpnetwork.org

FAB Parents

Offers resources and online training for adoptive and foster parents of trauma-triggered children and the professionals who touch their lives.

Website: www.fabparents.co.uk

Family Action (Formally PAC.UK)

Providing practical, emotional and financial support through community services to those who are experiencing poverty, disadvantage and social isolation.

Website: www.family-action.org.uk

FRG (Family Rights Group)

Charity working with parents and family members in England and Wales with children at risk or in care, advising on legal rights and options when the courts and social care system is involved in decisions about children. Freephone 0808 801 0366.

Website: www.frg.org.uk

Gateway Psychology

Provides for the psychological needs of children, young people and families in the Stoke-on-Trent area and surrounding regions, specialising in working with children who are adopted and/or have suffered early trauma.

Website: www.gateway-psychology.co.uk

Email: contact@gateway-psychology.co.uk

Home Start

Volunteer support for families across England, Wales, Scotland and Northern Ireland through their toughest times.

Website: www.home-start.org.uk
Email: info@home-start.org.uk

IPSEA (Independent Parent Special Education Advice)

Free legally based advice to families who have children with special educational needs.
Website: www.ipsea.org.uk

National Association of Therapeutic Parents

To assist parents and professionals in gaining the specialist knowledge, skills and strategies required for effective Therapeutic Parenting.
Website: www.naotp.com

Partnership Projects

Expertise in psychological interventions for overcoming the effects of trauma, including trauma-focused therapy and non-violent restraint (NVR).
Website: www.partnershipsprojectsuk.com

St Francis' Children's Society

SFCS is committed to finding families for those children who wait longest in the care system before finding adoptive families.
Website: www.sfcs.org.uk
Email: enquiries@sfcs.org.uk

Take 3 Parenting

Helps practitioners develop skills and strategies for supporting parents to deal with challenging teenagers.
Website: www.take3parenting.co.uk
Email: info@take3parenting.co.uk

Tandem Carer Services

Expert advice for adopters, foster carers, special guardians and kinship carers, shared lives, staying put, special needs and disability carers. Advice, support and protection from allegations and excellent training to help carers protect themselves and feel safe in their homes.

Website: www.tandemservices.org

SOCIAL MEDIA/INTERNET BULLYING

Adopteens.org.uk

Online forum for anyone who is adopted, aged between 11 and 18 and lives within Yorkshire or Humber.

Website: www.adopteens.org.uk

Child Exploitation and Online Protection command

Are you worried about online sexual abuse or the way someone has been communicating with you online? Report and/or receive advice from a Child Protection Advisor here (part of the National Crime Agency).

Website: www.ceop.police.uk

Childline

If you are being bullied, or you are not ready to make a report to CEOP, you can talk to Childline anonymously online or on the phone. No worry is too big or too small.

Website: www.childline.org.uk

Freephone: 0800 1111

Childnet
Childnet International is a non-profit organisation working with others to help make the internet a great and safe place for children.
Website: www.childnet.com

Kidscape
Advice and support around bullying for young people and their parents and guardians.
Website: www.kidscape.org.uk
Email: info@kidscape.org.uk

HEALTH

BMA
The British Medical Association (BMA) represents, supports and negotiates on behalf of all UK doctors and medical students, lobbying and campaigning on the issues impacting the medical profession – useful to see what campaigns they are working on in regards to specific conditions such as foetal alcohol syndrome.
Website: www.bma.org.uk

Contact – For families with disabled children
Helping families and children with disabilities feel valued, supported and informed.
Website: www.contact.org.uk
Email: info@contact.org.uk

Cpotential
Works with babies, children and young people who have movement disorders due to conditions such as cerebral

palsy, global development delay or acquired brain injury, and associated learning disabilities or sensory processing/communication.
Website: www.Cpotential.org.uk

Disability Grants

Supporting parents or carers of a disabled child to identify suitable charities and trusts that provide funding towards the high cost of disability equipment, holidays, housing, days out, etc.
Website: www.disability-grants.org

First Aid For Life

First-aid courses and advice to help babies, children and teenagers. Practical and online courses for parents and child carers. Also mental health courses in partnership with Maudsley Learning (clinicians from Maudsley Hospital).
Website: www.firstaidforlife.org.uk

Freedom for Kids

Dedicated to helping families with disabled children seeking charitable funding or purchase equipment for your child/children.
Website: www.freedomforkids.co.uk

Heads Together

The mental health initiative spearheaded by the Royal Foundation of the Duke and Duchess of Cambridge, combining campaigning to tackle stigma and change the conversation around mental health with fundraising for new mental health services.
Website: www.headstogether.org.uk

National Organisation for Fetal Alcohol Spectrum Disorders

Helpful Facebook organisation and community bringing together FASD resources, campaigns and support.
Facebook: National FASD

New Life

Nursing support for families of disabled/ill children, plus campaigning and fundraising for equipment to change a child's life.
Website: www.newlifecharity.co.uk

Rainbow Trust

Providing bespoke support for families who have a child with a serious illness.
Website: www.rainbowtrust.org.uk

St John Ambulance

First aid advice for children and babies including choking, croup, drowning, head injuries, hypothermia, how to do a primary survey, CPR and the recovery position.
Website: www.sja.org.uk

WellChild

Making it possible for children and young people across the UK with exceptional health needs to be cared for at home instead of hospital, wherever possible.
Website: www.wellchild.org.uk

Young Minds

The UK's leading charity for children and young people's mental health.
Website: www.youngminds.org.uk

READING

Bessel van der Kolk, *The Body Keeps the Score: Mind, brain and body in the transformation of trauma* (Penguin, 2015)

Betsy de Thierry, *A Simple Guide to Attachment Difficulties in Children* (Jessica Kingsley Publishers, 2019)

PODCASTS

Adopted Feels
100 per cent real talk with two Korean adoptee besties Hana and Ryan, Korean adoptees from Melbourne, Australia, who talk about anything and everything adoption-related, including race, gender, birth family search and reunion, and more.
Website: www.adopted-feels.simplecast.com

Adoptees On
A community filled with resilient and passionate adult adoptees with insightful, informative and validating conversation.
Website: www.adopteeson.com

Adoption: The Long View
LavenderLuz.com is where Lori Holden, honoured by the US Congress as an 'Angel in Adoption', explores the complexities of adoption from many viewpoints and interviews adoption thought leaders.
Website: www.lavenderluz.com

The Adoption
Radio 4 podcast telling the story of a UK adoption through the eyes of those affected.
Website: www.bbc.co.uk/programmes/p05k3wsq

April Dinwoodie
'As a transracially adopted person (I am brown, adopted into a white family) raised in a predominately white environment, I live a life where it is imperative that I gracefully and safely move through circumstances and situations related to differences of race, class and culture.'
Website: www.aprildinwoodie.com

Frontline: 'Stories of Change'
Frontline's new podcast, 'Stories of Change', speaks to amazing people and organisations whose mission is to bring about social change and make a real difference to the lives of vulnerable children and families.
Website: www.thefrontline.org.uk/stories-of-change

'Who Am I Really?'
Damon L. Davis shares his journey through life as an adoptee to becoming an adoptive parent himself.
Website: www.whoamireallypodcast.com

ACKNOWLEDGEMENTS

I am not an expert, I don't believe anyone is. With a lot of work we can become specialists but we always need to confer with others to enrich our knowledge. I need to thank the following for their time, wisdom and support:

My family who feature in all my books (this time only tea, coffee and cake was required); Andy Wills (University of Plymouth); Nick Reeve (University of Portsmouth); Jayne Saul Paterson, adult BAME adoptee and professional career coach; Heather Maddox, adopter and social worker; Maria Osbourne, post-adoption social worker; Tandem Carer Services; Becky Poole, adopter; Jocelyn and Coco Sartain, adopter and adoptee; Abraham and V, adopter and adoptee; Sakeetha, Matt, J and K, adopters and adoptees; Oliver and his adoptive son; Kate Swann and Margert Allen for second and third reading; Lisa Haines, accountant; Ruth Marriot, CEO of Families For Children; Fay, Police Child Protection Officer; Samantha Davidson, deputy head teacher; Elizabeth Davies, SENCo.

I owe the greatest thanks to a man I never knew.

At nine years old, I went on a school trip to the Tate Gallery. A small crowd had gathered round the Carl Andre, *Equivalent VIII* (aka Bricks) sculpture. I stood there invisibly, or so I thought, and listened to the adults talk about the work: 'Is it art?'. I had never heard such a conversation and was fascinated. An American, who I thought was a beautiful hippy-looking man, spoke so knowingly about art. I was both fascinated and terrified. I was in this incredible building feeling, as I usually did, that I was not entitled to anything. Then the man looked directly at me and said, 'Art is for everyone'. There are some adults who are able to 'see' children, to intuitively understand and recognise their souls; these adults give generously and want nothing in return. That glorious man changed my life, because after he said that it dawned on me that I was an everyone.

I became an artist.

INDEX